MONEY

FOR
NOTHING

Ten Great Ways
to Make Money
illegally

Money for Nothing:
Ten Great Ways to Make Money Illegally
By Jeremy Mercer

©1999 Jeremy Mercer

ISBN: 1-894020-63-4
Published by Warwick Publishing
162 John Street, Toronto, Ontario M5V 2E5
Canada
www.warwickgp.com

Design: Heidi Gemmill
Illustrations: Rob Cross
Editor: Melinda Tate

Printed and bound in Canada

MONEY
FOR
NOTHING

Ten Great Ways
to Make Money
illegally

jeremy mercer

Warwick Publishing
Toronto   Los Angeles
www.warwickgp.com

TABLE OF CONTENTS

PREFACE

This is neither a work of journalism nor fiction, but rather an experiment in story-telling.

Over the past three years, I've been lucky enough to meet dozens of fascinating people who happen to make their money on the wrong side of the law. These pages hold ten of their stories.

In each person's case, I've taken some measures to obscure their identity. This has not been done solely for reasons of privacy, but for very real legal concerns as well. Some of my sources are still before the courts, some have confessed to past crimes for which they've not yet been caught, and some continue to earn their daily bread through decidedly illegal activity.

As a result, in certain cases, all I've done is dropped a person's last name or changed their first. In others, I've altered minor details of their lives and their crimes to better protect them. And in a few cases, I've gone so far as to transplant the characters into different cities altogether.

My role in these stories varies as well. Where it is unavoidable and central to the plot, my first-person observations are included. Other stories are told strictly through the subjects' own words, while in a couple chapters I have hidden myself and describe acts and conversations that took place before me.

Each chapter is based on interviews and events that I have either witnessed or confirmed through police sources. I believe I have remained faithful to these people's stories and that what follows is an authentic accounting of their lives and struggles. The result, I hope, is an interesting look at a handful of people who live on society's fringe.

ACKNOWLEDGEMENTS

Sometimes my life is so scattered, it seems a miracle that I can make it to work in the morning on time and fully clothed. When it comes to a project as daunting as this book, it is truly amazing that it comes together at all. I constantly find myself wondering, How did this get done? Then I remember. I had a lot of help from a lot of good, good people.

First, there are my friends and colleagues at the *Ottawa Citizen*. A tip of the hat to the men in charge at the paper, Neil Reynolds and Scott Anderson. They continue to give young reporters incredible opportunities that can't be had elsewhere in Canadian journalism. As for my immediate bosses, Randy Boswell and Ric Davey: I still have no idea how you can show such astounding patience, but I am grateful for it. And for my partner at the courthouse, Peter Hum, there is nobody better to work with.

Good friends like Paula McCooey kept me sane through the whole process, while the esteemed Dave Ebner added his usual creative insights. Talented young lawyers like Will Murray and James Foord helped keep it all in perspective, while Michael Woloschuk shared my anguish as he struggled to write his second book at the very same time. And for Harmen Meinders: Thanks for taking me through the final exhausting leg.

Of course, nothing in my life would be possible without the love and support of my parents, Ross and Patricia Mercer. A son couldn't ask for more.

For all those intriguing folk who helped me but that I can't name for legal reasons, the next round is on me.

Finally, to Jim, Nick, Melinda and Heidi at Warwick Publishing, thanks for giving me another chance to write for you and for bringing it all together.

INTRODUCTION

During an interview a couple of years ago, Yves told me no matter what happened in his life, one of the things he would never do was walk into a bank with a gun.

It's for fools, he explained. First, you never make any real money. Banks keep the majority of their funds in time-lock safes at the back. All that's available is a couple thousand in the tellers' tills. Second, it's simply a stupid crime. The banks have cameras, tellers trained to remember a person's physical details, and instant-reaction alarm systems wired straight to the cop shop. Even worse, most banks use dye bombs—little pouches of indelible ink that explode five minutes after being activated. Tellers throw the dye bombs in with the cash, and while the robber is making his getaway, it bursts, ruining the money and maybe even marking up the would-be bandit.

Then there are all the people in the bank: customers, tellers, managers—all are witnesses, and even worse, potential victims if something goes wrong. A gun is a wild card. You never know what's going to happen inside a bank and if you're forced to shoot, somebody might get hurt, which someone like Yves doesn't want, either on his conscience or his record. Finally, if you do get pinched by police, you get pinched hard. The courts come down severely on armed robbers: It's a crime of violence.

Yves added it up for me. The upside? You get maybe three or four thousand dollars. The downside? You're going to be caught on videotape, there are going to be witnesses, you've got to deal with the bank's security measures, and if you do get popped, you're looking at hard time because judges hate guns.

"You'd have to be sick to try it," Yves told me. "You can't be stupid. There are good ways to make money out there, but kid, you gotta remember, there are bad ways too."

I have to admit, I respected Yves a little bit more after that. I liked knowing there were lines he wouldn't cross.

And for me, it was the first time I'd actually thought about that—good crimes and bad crimes; smart crimes and stupid crimes. Before that, I'd always viewed the law in more absolute terms: If something's illegal, it's bad.

Of course, I wasn't naïve. Everybody rationalizes minor violations. Who hasn't dallied in recreational drugs at some point? Who hasn't taken home a few extra supplies from work? Who hasn't broken the speed limit or fudged on an insurance claim? There are certain laws that a large number of otherwise law-abiding citizens, after some thought and debate, choose to ignore. Who am I hurting by smoking a little dope before the Bob Dylan concert?

Who am I hurting if I pay the plumber in cash and save ten per cent? Most people can cross the line and still sleep well at night.

What Yves taught me is that the same rationalization works in the criminal world. Those who break the law for a living are keenly aware of both the Criminal Code and the moods of the courts. For the smart ones, crimes of violence are far less acceptable than so-called "victimless crimes." Violence instigates more intense police investigations, leads to stiffer penalties, and, if the perpetrator has any conscience at all, leaves a sour taste in the mouth.

There was no better person to learn all of this from than Yves. He was a member of the notorious Champagne Gang, a group of four young men who traveled across Canada and broke into more than a hundred drug stores and shopping malls at night in order to clean out their safes. They were master thieves who netted between two and six million dollars over their six-year crime spree, depending on whose estimates you believe. When they were finally caught, the gang received the incredibly light sentence of just two-years-less-a-day in jail.

Yves and the gang were the subject of my first book, *The Champagne Gang*. While researching that book, I spent a lot of time with them. And to my surprise, they each turned out to be intelligent, fun, spirited men, the kind of guys with whom you'd love to spend an evening drinking beer and swapping stories. Sure, they had a different perspective on right and wrong, but they weren't that bad. They never hurt anybody, they never violated a private home, and they never used a weapon of any sort. Simply put, I liked them.

Since I wrote that book in 1997, I've visited more crime scenes and sat in on scores of criminal trials in my role as a crime reporter for the *Ottawa Citizen*. During that time, I've met dozens of "criminals"—men and women charged with everything from stealing a bassoon to defrauding a bank of more than $50,000 to murdering a man. Because of the job, I also was lucky enough to meet another handful of characters who dealt drugs, smuggled cigarettes and performed an assortment of other illegal acts, but had not yet been caught by police.

What I quickly learned is what Yves had been telling me all along: Some of these people are *good* people. While I didn't condone their offences, some bothered me less than others. When I interviewed a man convicted of trading child porn, my stomach turned. But the man whose tax rebate scam netted him more than $1 million? Not that bad a guy. The little creeps who busted a beer bottle over a man's head, putting him in a coma and forcing him to undergo a frontal lobotomy? I'd cross the street to avoid them. But the laid-back, hippie marijuana grower? A great guy to have a coffee with.

With Yves's words about good crimes and bad crimes lodged in my mind, this book idea was born. In an era where law-and-order types would like to build a Super Jail on every corner and give 12-year-old boys penitentiary terms, I think it's important to remember that regular people, *good* people, end up on the wrong side of the law too. Every man or woman who appears before a judge is somebody's son or daughter, or mother or father for that matter.

What follows are stories about ten people I've met who I consider to be "good" criminals. Among them are a marijuana grower, a bookie, a dominatrix and a smuggler.

I've chosen these people not just because I found them to be generally decent people, but because their crimes were, in my mind, not that intrusive or harmful.

Sure, a marijuana grower is breaking the law, but he is only supplying an eager market. I don't see him as that different than Bacardi or Molson or du Maurier. Distilleries and breweries and cigarette makers just happen to work within the law. Likewise, a bookie and a drug dealer never profit off innocent people: Their customers are well aware of their addictions and how to feed them. And while a credit card fraud may steal from VISA and a smuggler may deprive the government of tax dollars, I'd rather they made their money that way than by breaking into my parents' home. As for the dominatrix—well, trust me: She isn't hurting anybody who doesn't want to be hurt.

It isn't surprising to me that the legal system often views these people in the same light. While pedophiles and armed robbers are dealt with harshly, the type of people who are found in these pages are treated with a bit more respect. If caught, the punishment faced by those in this book is often measured in dollars instead of days in jail. When a fine isn't acceptable and imprisonment is in order, it's usually very short terms at treatment centres or medium-security jails. Despite the fact that they've earned some good money in their days, these people will not be spending any time at the Kingston Penitentiary.

As I tell these people's stories, I have taken steps to cloak their true identity. I do this for several reasons. In some cases, the people are still before the courts and what they have told me could aid in their conviction. In other cases, they have already been through the court system but have told me about crimes for which they have never been prosecuted.

And finally, several of these people are still in business, earning their living without any complications from police. For me to identify them would likely lead to their being charged. One man, whom I've called Ian, told me about a safe job he pulled off for more than $100,000. That crime has never been solved. Before we started talking, I assured him his identity would be protected. He seemed to trust me, but just to make a point, he reminded me how easy it was for somebody to get away with an aggravated assault. If somebody wearing a balaclava comes up to you and beats you with a baseball bat, how are you ever going to identify them? he would ask me (hypothetically, of course). It wasn't a direct threat, but I got the point. These people generously gave me their time. I should respect the promises of anonymity I made to them.

One last note: As part of this work, I've included detailed descriptions of how these men and women commit their crimes. I'm aware this might trigger some criticism, but I've found that people want to know how these things are done and I believe they have the right to know. If knowledge is indeed power, then I don't see why the bad guys should have exclusive access to this sort of information.

Certainly, this book might give insight into criminal activities to those who might use the information for illegal purposes. I don't doubt that there will be a teenager or two who will learn how to cut drugs or scam a credit card from these pages. But the fact remains that by and large, most people with the will to commit a crime already have the way. To those who already inhabit the criminal world, there is nothing new in these pages. And to those who are led into the criminal world by this book, they would have likely ended up there anyway, albeit with a different guide. All this book does is tell people what the bad guys already know.

THE SUN IS THE WORLD'S GROW LIGHT: THE ART OF MARIJUANA CULTIVATION

It's noon when I get the message from Simon.

He had left it at about 10:30 that morning. I had been out running some errands at the time, fixing the rearview mirror on my car, getting some money from the bank, picking up dry-cleaning—the usual stuff. It's the third Wednesday of March, St. Patrick's Day as it happens, and I've taken a vacation day from work. When I get back to the apartment, the message light is flashing.

"Jeremy. It's Simon. I need a lawyer."

My heart jumps. I sit on the couch and play the message again, searching for answers in his voice. Obviously, the message can only mean one thing: Something bad has happened. The question is: How bad? The sun streams through the window of my apartment as I mull over the situation.

The first thing to do is to call Steve, another one of the people who help Simon at "the Co-Op." He's a young guy, 23, working as a sales rep at a downtown HMV record store. It being a Wednesday morning, the store is dead quiet, so Steve slips into the back room where he can talk freely.

"Look, have you heard anything from Simon?" I ask.

"No. Why? What's up?"

"I just . . . Look, I just got a message from him. He says he needs a lawyer. I think something's happened to the Co-Op."

"What? What does the message say?" There's real alarm in his voice.

"That's it. It just says he needs a lawyer."

Steve is silent on the other line. He whistles softly between his teeth and I can picture him, tugging at his ponytail, his eyes suddenly alert. Finally, he answers.

"Shit. Randy"—Steve is talking about the other member of the Co-Op—"is out of town. He'd know what to do. I'll try to track him down. I'll make some calls."

I tell him that, in the meantime, I'm going to try and check out the situation. He warns me to be careful and hangs up. When Simon, Randy and Steve allowed me to sit in on their marijuana growing operation—the Co-Op as they called it—I swore to a list of rules: Never talk about locations; never talk about names; and never talk about anything on the phone. Steve would probably be angry I called, even though we spoke only in vague terms. But what the hell—this was serious.

I lock up my apartment and take the building's stairs two at a time to where my Jetta is parked on Frank Street. I have to confirm what Steve and I already know in our hearts: Simon has been picked up by the police.

When I used to try and envision what a small-time drug czar would look like, I never pictured Simon. He's a smallish man, maybe five foot eight, with the gift of dark hair and olive skin from his Portuguese parents. He'd recently turned 43, but depending on his mood, he could look anywhere from 30 to 50. His thick, wire-rimmed glasses always sat crookedly on his nose and his wide smile was tarnished only by tobacco-stained teeth.

Ever since I'd met Simon, he'd always seemed happy and always had something good to say about something or someone. He was a boundless source of optimism, though everything he said came out in a clipped accent. English was his third language, after Portuguese and French, and it meant his words were delivered with a touch of hesitation.

When I got the message on St. Patrick's Day, I had known Simon for about a year-and-a-half. In that time he had grown more than 30 kilos of marijuana and built the city's biggest medical marijuana operation. For a young newspaper reporter, he was a good man to know.

Simon had had a tumultuous, life-long love affair with drugs, but it was the medical marijuana network that was his current pride and joy. He even went so far as to refer to the marijuana plants as his children.

The network was an underground community that hooked up dozens of ailing cancer and AIDS patients with a reliable supply of high-quality marijuana. If a sick person could provide a doctor's note testifying that marijuana helped their illness, or could show Simon a real medical need on his or her own, he made sure that man or woman was provided with affordable marijuana.

For R.J., an AIDS patient whose appetite was destroyed by medication, Simon provided Kush, a nice, smooth strain of marijuana that inspired an incredible appetite—"the Super Munchies" as Simon called it; a few tokes of this pot could make any man or woman hungry enough to put an all-you-can-eat Chinese buffet out of business.

Gerard, who had the beginnings of Parkinson's disease, preferred Freezeland, a calming strain of marijuana that put its user in an ultra-mellow state of mind. For certain Parkinson's patients, Gerard included, the pot helps reduce the shakes and trembles that torture the body.

And for Barb, who was undergoing twice-monthly chemotherapy, it was Silver Pearl, a smoke she found settled her stomach and chased away nausea.

"Whatever works, whatever works," Simon would mutter as he carved up the different buds of marijuana and placed them into tiny plastic bags for distribution.

By the mid-1990s, the medical benefits of marijuana were widely accepted and networks like the one Simon built were already in place in most major North American cities. Simon got involved in the Ottawa scene in 1996, and, as is so often the case with such things, it was only because of a bizarre twist of fate.

For Simon, drugs had been a way of life since he was 15. First, as a teenager growing up in Portugal, he ran hash between Morocco and Europe. When he moved to Montreal with his brother in the early 1970s, he began smuggling sheets of LSD from labs in Quebec across the American border and down to Boston and Vermont. By the time he was 30, he was a serious veteran of the drug trade and was proud of the fact he'd only been busted once— selling a pound of hash to an undercover police officer in Laval.

"You know what got me about this guy," Simon said. "He was so *short!* I never thought a short guy like that could be a cop. I thought they had a height restriction or something . . . Hey, you learn something everyday, right?"

```
Marijuana Possession: The Legalities

THE NARCOTIC CONTROL ACT (CANADA)

Possession of a Narcotic:

(1) Except as authorized by this act or the regulations,
    no person shall have a narcotic in his possession.

(2) Every person who contravenes subsection (1) is guilty
    of an offence and liable
    (a) on summary conviction for first offence, to a
        fine not exceeding one thousand dollars or to
        imprisonment for a term not exceeding six months
        or both.
    (b) on conviction by indictment, to imprisonment
        for a term not exceeding seven years.
```

By his early 30s, Simon had tired of the covert smuggling operations and high-tension border crossings, so he turned to his first love: marijuana. Not only had it always been his drug of choice, but he had a green thumb and quickly became known for some of the best marijuana in Quebec. He had a knack for producing bountiful, mind-bending crops in just a five-and-a-half-week grow time—an incredible turn-around time for an indoor operation. His grow rooms were scattered across Montreal and his profits let him travel as much as he wanted.

But as Simon's reputation grew in Quebec, it began to cause him some problems. Before he moved to Ottawa in the late '80s, Simon fielded a dozen offers from the Hell's Angels to become an official grower for them. It was one of the cushiest gigs in the business: guaranteed cash salary of about $100,000 a year, the clout of the Hells to keep people from ripping you off, and usually, a pretty sweet deal with local law enforcement officials to ignore the activities in your grow rooms.

Yet Simon always turned down the feelers from the Hells; he hated their tactics. All they were concerned with was getting the most marijuana grown in the least amount of time. Simon cared about the plants. Simon loved the plants. He wanted to grow rare exotic varieties, he wanted to experiment with growing plants from seeds, he wanted to fiddle around with everything from the carbon-dioxide level in the air to the temperature of the water in the hydroponics system. He dreamt of growing the perfect pot.

The Hells—they didn't give a rat's ass about quality. If a couple of extra days of growing would make the pot sweeter, they didn't care; the sooner you cut, the sooner you could start growing your next crop. Even worse, if a crop got hit with an insect infestation, the gangs would insist on spraying the whole thing down with Raid. It was one of the few things that made Simon really angry.

"People are smoking that shit, and they don't care, they just spray whatever, do whatever," he said, his arms waving in the air, ashes flying off of his cigarette. "I won't do that. I won't touch that. It's not for me."

When Simon got a bug infestation—it was usually aphids that hit the marijuana—he delicately sprayed every plant with a mixture of water and liquid soap each day for a week. It took longer and it wasn't as effective as the chemicals, but Simon wouldn't dream of using pesticides.

As for the money—money wasn't an issue for Simon: no wife, no kids, no mortgage. He already made more than he could spend.

So, when the Hells started to get a bit sensitive about having their offer rejected so many times, Simon came to Ottawa in 1995 rather than risk the wrath of Quebec's most violent motorcycle gang.

In Ottawa, he started out by growing small crops in the basements of rented homes. There were usually three or four on the go at any one time, and if everything went as planned, it brought in upwards of $10,000 every month. It was a good life. Once he deducted costs—equipment, electricity, the occasional crop lost to thieves—he could usually count on a profit of about $3,000 or $4,000 a month. Not bad for doing what he loved.

Simon was a happy and wealthy man. He could make regular visits back to Portugal to visit his parents, he was looking at a nice farm he wanted to buy, and he was thinking about using some of the money to open a Portuguese bar. A life-long bachelor, Simon was even considering finding a steady woman. He was content.

Then he met R.J.

The two were old friends but hadn't seen each other for more than a decade. They'd first met years ago, back in Montreal in the early '80s. At that time they knew each other from the local scene, and the two became friends. R.J. was like most in his crowd—he liked to party, he liked to experiment. One of those experiments involved injecting various drugs into his veins. He only went down that path a couple of times, but that was all it took. A dirty needle gave him the virus.

Back then, in the early '80s, R.J. had weighed 135 pounds. He weighed just 85 pounds when Simon bumped into him again in September 1996. They met at a Hull hospital, Simon there to visit a friend with a collapsed lung, R.J. there to die of AIDS.

R.J. was on serious medication—more than 30 pills a day—to combat the virus. But he couldn't keep them down. The pills made him too sick to eat and he was wasting away to nothing. R.J. was 33 in July 1996. He'd bottomed out at 75 pounds and his doctor had given him three months to live.

They'd like to give the world a toke ...

There's enough marijuana grown in Canada every year to get more than a quarter of the world high, at least for an afternoon.

According to estimates by the Royal Canadian Mounted Police, there are roughly 800 tonnes of marijuana grown every year. Each tonne represents 1,000 kilograms, which means more than 800 million grams of marijuana are grown in Canada each year. Since you can roll roughly two joints out of each gram, that's an incredible 1.6 billion joints a year—enough for more than one out of every four people on Earth.

Still, R.J. was a sport. He figured he was going to die soon, so he might as well spend the last months doing what he loved. For the first time since he'd been diagnosed with AIDS, R.J. went back to drugs, rolling himself a big joint out of a baggie his wife had snuck into the hospital.

Then a funny thing happened. He felt hungry. He could eat again. And when he ate, he could keep the food down. With regular smoking, in two months he'd gained 10 pounds and R.J.'s doctor had changed his prognosis from three months to live to three years to live. Things were good. Well, at least better.

That September day in 1996 when they were reunited in the Hull hospital, R.J. confided to his old friend Simon how hard it was to get marijuana. He didn't have a set dealer, so his wife had to go to bars or the Rideau Centre, the big mall downtown, to score. Then, he was paying street prices of $12 to $15 a gram. He and his wife lived on social assistance and the marijuana expenses were taking a financial toll.

The worst part was that R.J. never knew what he was getting. Sometimes, he'd get weak, low-grade marijuana that gave him a bad buzz and a pounding headache. Other times, it'd be such powerful dope it would put him on the couch all day. R.J. told Simon there were dozens of other patients in the same boat as him.

For Simon, the seed for the Co-Op was planted.

$ $ $

When I go flying by the police cruiser, I realize I'm driving way too fast. I slow down and give the constable a contrite wave in the newly fixed rearview mirror. Miraculously, he doesn't pull me over, even though I was doing a good 110 in a 70 zone. Maybe it's a sign.

I'm heading up to Chelsea, a scenic Quebec town about 15 minutes north

WHO's Kidding Who?

In early 1998, Britain's *New Scientist* magazine reported that officials at the World Health Organization in Geneva had suppressed findings that cannabis is safer than alcohol or tobacco. Spokespersons for WHO said it dropped the findings because of contradictions, and that the "conclusions were not scientifically sound." But the magazine reported there are lingering suspicions that the WHO buckled under political pressure from certain countries that feared the findings would fuel the growing fight to legalize marijuana.

of Ottawa. Half of it was built around the rivers and lakes that surrounded the Camp Fortune ski hill. This was the predominantly English and richer half of town. The other half was built along the Gatineau River. That was the predominantly French and poorer half. It was along the banks of the Gatineau that Simon had his newest marijuana operation.

One of Simon's patients, a woman named Sylvia, moved to Chelsea after being diagnosed with cancer. She didn't want to live the rest of her life in a city, so here she is in a little white house on a couple acres of land with clean air and a huge vegetable garden out back. She loves it. There's a mini-apartment in the basement of the white house and, with Sylvia's approval, Simon had converted it into a grow room just three months earlier. It is this grow room, which Simon liked to call "the Farm," that I had become involved in. And now my gut tells me it is this grow room that has been busted by the police.

Simon's message keeps on running through my head as I drive. *Jeremy. It's Simon. I need a lawyer.* His voice had sounded anxious, but not scared. He had to have been taken in by the police. Why else would he need a lawyer? For the good of the operation, I hope he's been stopped while driving and that police had only found him holding a couple of ounces of marijuana. Then the cops would be able to nail him with possession or possession for the purpose of trafficking. But it would mean the grow rooms were safe.

The worst case would be if the cops had stumbled onto one or more of his operations. Along with the newly created Farm in Chelsea, Simon had three other setups—one in Ottawa, one in Hull, and one in Nepean. If all four have been busted, it could prove fatal for the medical marijuana network.

I take the Macdonald-Cartier Bridge over the Ottawa River, which separates Eastern Ontario and Western Quebec. It's 1 p.m. and the traffic is light. Everyone is at work, in school or at home. Whatever cars are on Highway 5 take the exit to the Hull Casino. There isn't anybody else in sight when the sign for Chelsea appears. I slide my Jetta down the ramp and turn towards the Farm.

Marijuana Made to Measure

The marijuana business uses a hybrid of metric and imperial for its measurements. The base unit is always the gram. But as you move up, you deal in ounces, which are 28 grams, pounds, which are 454 grams, and then you top out at kilos, which are 1,000 grams. It makes for interesting negotiations and calculations. In the U.S., it's also sold by the dollar amount: a "dimer' is simply $10 worth of marijuana, the actual weight of which can vary considerably.

My plan is to walk nonchalantly up to the house and ring the doorbell or peek in the window. I can't get arrested for that—at least that's what I tell myself. If I do run into a cop, I can just flash my press credentials and explain I'm a journalist working on a story.

I drive slowly past the Farm to scout out the situation. There's a strange Chevy Caprice parked in the driveway and a minivan parked about 50 metres down the road. No marked police cars, no yellow police tape. I drive for another kilometre or so, do a U-turn, and then pull into the Farm's gravel driveway, parking next to the mystery Chevy.

When I open the car door, I'm hit with the smell of fresh marijuana. You usually get this smell in the Farm's tropical grow room, but not outside. I wander around to the back door. I hear crashing and the sound of breaking glass from inside. A heavyset cop is standing guard. He wears the colours of the Royal Canadian Mounted Police drug squad.

"What do you want?" he barks, his French accent thick.

I pull out my business card. "I'm from the newspaper. I heard there was a bust here—"

The cop waves the back of his hand at me before I can finish. "Get out of here. Call headquarters later."

I nod and walk away, my heart doing a lightning beat. This is a most unwanted development.

$ $ $

When I first met Simon in November 1997, I never imagined I would end up watching the man grow marijuana.

It was more than a year after he'd renewed his acquaintance with R.J., and his medical marijuana network was going full tilt. I was a crime reporter for the local newspaper, the *Ottawa Citizen*, and I was assigned to write a feature on the city's medical marijuana community. After a little research, I learned that Simon was at the head of it all. It took a week to track him down, but when we finally met, we hit it off. He agreed to an interview and later gave me a tour of his operation. I even spent a day with him delivering marijuana to patients across the city. That was the day he told me about R.J. and how the network got started.

When Simon met R.J. in September 1996, he said it was like a calling. Here was a challenge he could embrace: Grow marijuana for those who need it and craft the plants to meet the specific needs of a specific patient. As he ran the numbers at home that night, Simon realized everybody could be a winner with this deal.

When you broke it down, it cost Simon about $2 to produce a gram of marijuana. That figure included the cost of the hydroponic system, rent for the apartment or the house, electricity to run the lamps, and other assorted fertilizers and tools. Usually, Simon sold his marijuana for between $1,500 and $3,500 a pound to mid-level dealers who distributed the drug either on the street or to regular customers.

Like most commodities, the price for marijuana is in constant flux. In the late '90s it would fall to between $1,500 and $2,000 in the fall and winter when the market was flooded with an abundance of marijuana grown outdoors over the summer. But in the spring and summer, when the outdoor supply was long gone and all that was left is indoor, hydroponically grown weed, the price shot up to between $3,000 and $3,500 a pound.

For Simon, that worked out to a sales price of between $4 and $8 a gram, depending on the time of year. Since it cost him $2 to produce, his profit was between $2 and $6 a gram, a potential income of $4,000 to $12,000 a month if he was able to produce at least two kilos of quality marijuana each month.

The problem for guys like R.J. was that the same marijuana that Simon sold to the mid-level dealer for $4 to $8 a gram cost between $12 and $15 on the street, depending on how many hands it passed through to get to the customer and how much profit each handler wanted. With those margins, Simon figured he could do the right thing and still earn a good living.

Hunched over his desk that night, a pencil and calculator in hand, Simon decided he could manage to sell marijuana as low as $3.50 a gram to patients. If he met his minimum production target of 2,000 grams a month, at a profit of $1.50 a gram, that would still be a monthly income of $3,000, tax-free. As for the patients, they'd be saving $8.50 to $11.50 a gram off street prices and be getting a quality, reliable source of marijuana. Simon had indeed found his calling.

"How much food can you eat? How many shoes do you need?" said Simon, dismissing the drop in income. "I still make my money, a lot of it. I'm not *that* good of a guy."

After working the numbers out, he called R.J. with the idea. The ground rules were simple: you had to be sick to qualify for the discount price; you had to have either your doctor's approval or demonstrate your need to Simon; and no matter what, you could never resell the discount marijuana to make money for yourself.

R.J. agreed to the rules, and so did about a dozen other patients he knew. Just like that, Simon was hooked into a fringe medical community. The patients that scored the good marijuana off Simon told other patients,

patients told doctors, and soon, Simon was providing marijuana directly to doctors for distribution.

Simon was now producing about 2,400 grams a month for the medical marijuana network. About 1,500 grams were going to a group of roughly 50 patients in Eastern Ontario and Western Quebec, each of whom received an average "prescription" of a gram a day, or 30 grams a month. The last part of the crop, roughly 900 grams, was sent to a collective of doctors in Montreal.

"I could grow twice as much and still not have enough. The ones in Montreal, they always need more and here, every day I get another call or hear about somebody else," Simon said.

After I met him and toured his operation, I ended up writing a series of newspaper stories about Simon, the medical marijuana network, and the battle to legalize the drug for medicinal purposes. In the months that followed, Simon and I stayed in touch. He was a good source to have and a genuinely nice guy. I watched as he became intimate with most of Canada's medical marijuana crusaders. He began actively following the legal battles raging in Toronto, London, and Vancouver to have the drug legalized for medical purposes. In Ottawa, he became a bit of a cult hero.

In December 1998, a little more than a year after we first met, Simon invited me over for a coffee and something to smoke. He wanted to know if I was interested in learning more about the marijuana business. He wanted to know if I would consider sitting in on his next grow operation, one he was planning for a little house in Chelsea. I jumped at the chance.

$ $ $

There were going to be four people involved in this particular marijuana operation: Simon, the marijuana expert and mastermind behind the project; Steve, the kid from HMV who made marijuana deliveries to patients for Simon and helped take care of the crops; Randy, an old hippie Simon knew who ran a café on Bank Street and baked marijuana muffins for cancer patients during his spare time; and me.

Even with Simon's great track record, I felt a bit nervous about joining the enterprise. The deal was that I would make a small donation to Simon to cover his time and buy him a new set of grow lights, but I wouldn't profit from the operation in any way. Still, my guess was that if something bad went down, a police officer might not be enthralled by my story.

The operation was going to start in January 1999. Simon signed the lease for the basement of the Chelsea house under a false name and got a pay-as-you-go cellular phone for the apartment. Nothing could be traced.

It was an ideal setup, Simon explained. With Sylvia upstairs, she could act as a lookout to make sure nobody suspicious came to the house. Her two yappy lap dogs, Fluff and Mighty Mite, ensured that nobody could sneak up on the house since they went into a barking frenzy every time somebody even set foot in the driveway.

The electricity situation was good too. A marijuana grower always has to be careful about their power bill. Grow lights use up a huge amount of electricity and a big jump in the bill is a tell-tale sign to authorities that somebody's growing. Simon wanted to run 4000 watts out of the new house. That meant four, 1000-watt grow lights, each of which could produce about a pound of marijuana every six weeks. Four grow lights used about $220 in electricity every two months. Simon called Hydro Quebec to get the average bi-monthly bill at the apartment and it averaged out to about $120 every two months. If Simon just threw down the lights, the bill would soar to $340 a month—an eye-popping jump.

Still, Simon assured me: "I can work this."

First, he "stole" the electricity for one of the lights—1000 watts—from Sylvia's house. He plugged the light into the outlet for her clothes dryer and paid her cash. That way, part of the electricity jump showed up on Sylvia's bill, not his, and it wouldn't draw much attention.

Then Simon "fixed" the apartment. He unplugged all the appliances, turned down the temperature on the hot water tank, and disconnected the baseboard heaters. The warmth coming off the grow lamps would more than compensate. When you added the fact that nobody actually lived there—no hot showers, no television, no computers—Simon figured the bill would be about $200 every two months—a mere $80 jump.

"That's not too bad. Maybe whoever lives here, they like to take a lot of showers. Maybe they're running the laundry all the time. I can live with it," Simon said as he worked the numbers for the tenth time on his calculator.

Pleased with the setup, Simon began preparing the grow room on January 24, 1999, coincidentally, my birthday.

Simon always liked to say that the sun was just the world's biggest grow light. Grown outside, marijuana plants go through a rapid growth cycle in the spring and steady growth during the summer. When the light changes at the end of the summer, it tells the plant winter's coming and it's time to reproduce. That's when a marijuana plant starts to grow its flowers, or "buds" as they're known. This is the end goal of any marijuana grower because the bud has the most THC—the psychoactive component that gives the user the high. While a marijuana plant may stand six feet tall and have a couple of pounds of leaves and branches on it, the only valuable part is the roughly 40 grams of bud that might be getting ready to blossom on each plant in the early fall.

For an indoor growing operation, you need grow lights to mimic the sun. It's an amazing operation that can shrink the natural, five-month growth period for marijuana to just six weeks.

Simon likes to use two types of lights. First, a metal-halide light, which costs about $70 per bulb. This light replicates the whiter light of spring and gives the plants their early season growth spurt. Then, you need a more gentle light that will act as the light of summer and early fall. This can be had through a high pressure sodium light that sells for about $75 per bulb. The bulbs can be bought at any hydroponics shop. Some growers just use the summer bulb and forgo the early season growth, but as Simon says, "it's a matter of taste."

The spring/summer light starts out on a cycle of 18 hours on, six hours off, to replicate the long days and short nights of late spring and early summer. After two weeks in the spring cycle, the bulb is changed, and the cycle is switched to 12 hours on, 12 hours off to represent the more even days and nights of late summer.

Before Simon actually installs grow lights in a room, he blocks the windows. Nothing is more suspicious to neighbours than the bright lights of a grow room that turn on and off at the exact same time every day. Likewise, you can't board up the windows because that's equally suspicious.

What Simon does is build "false fronts." For the basement apartment at the Farm, he filled the window looking down into the grow room with books, a vintage beer bottle, and other knickknacks. Then, he hammered an extra wood frame around the inside of the window that allowed him to staple a thick cloth curtain over the window. The final step was to run a wire into the space between the window and the cloth and have a small night light attached to that wire.

The light Simon left inside the false front was set on a separate timer and would go on and off about six times a day, giving the window a low glow, as if the light was on inside the room. Simon changed the timer's pattern once a week. With the books in the window and the light going on and off, it was enough for people to think it was a normal bedroom, albeit a bedroom with the curtains continuously drawn.

"It looks pretty good, eh?" Simon chuckled as he stood outside, joint in hand, admiring his handiwork.

I got the sense that Simon took the same pride in his false fronts as the window display designers do at Saks Fifth Avenue. Three times he went back inside to rearrange a book or add a couple of pens to his handiwork. The wood and cloth for the project cost Simon $15 and the timer $10.

Once the false front was built, Simon, Randy, and Steve spent the whole day washing and disinfecting the apartment. They wanted a clean environment and didn't dare risk the chance there might be some old soil or plant material that might be infested with bugs or disease. Once the place was washed down, they covered the walls with strips of white plastic. It took less than $20 worth to cover the entire, 20-by-20-foot room. Simon explained to me that the plastic helps contain the smell of the marijuana and the white surface reflects the light back onto the plants, giving them more growing power.

The next step was to set the power supply. Grow lights take so much energy that the regular current coming out of a wall socket can't give the lights enough juice to get started. For this, you need a ballast, which goes for about $120 alone, but is usually sold in conjunction with the lights and reflectors for about $500. The ballast is like a big battery that stores energy and builds up a powerful-enough charge to turn the lights on.

The floor of the Farm's grow room was divided into four quarters, one for each grow table. One light was hung in the centre of each quarter. With the lights in place, hanging from the ceiling, it was time to bring in the hydroponic systems.

Marijuana grows naturally in soil, but as Simon says, "all that does is hold the plant up." The plant feeds itself from the water and nutrients in the soil, so a hydroponic system bypasses the soil and delivers the water and nutrients directly to the roots of the plant.

There are two main types of hydro systems. The first is NFT—nutrient film technique. This system has long, eavestrough-type plastic channels, usu-

Marijuana and Health

In his 1992 book *Against Excess*, UCLA drug-policy scholar Mark Kleiman wrote: "Aside from the almost self-evident proposition that smoking anything is probably bad for the lungs, the quarter-century since large numbers of Americans began to use marijuana has produced remarkably little laboratory or epidemiological evidence of serious health damage done by the drug."

Simple comparison of the ratio of a substance's lethal dose to its effective dose seems to support that. For ASA (e.g., Aspirin), 10 to 20 times the effective dose can be lethal. For alcohol, just 4 to 10 times the effective dose can be lethal. And for marijuana? The ratio is 40,000 to 1.

ally six to eight feet long. The marijuana plants are put into small mesh pots, then surrounded by tiny clay pebbles to support the roots. These pots are then placed into holes on the top part of the eavestrough channel, leaving the plants suspended and the roots dangling into the trough. Water is continuously pumped through the channels of the trough from a water basin at one end of the operation, giving the plants a constant supply of food. The troughs are on a slight angle so the water drains back down into the basin below the troughs where the pump brings it back up again. The constant motion of the water creates oxygen for the roots and protects against rotting. The cost for one of these setups at any hydroponic store is about $250, including the pump to move the water, the troughs, and the tubes.

The other standard hydroponic setup is the ebb-and-flow system. In this case, you have a huge plastic tub, maybe four-by-four, raised off the ground. This tub is connected to a second tub on the ground filled with water and fertilizers. The marijuana plants are squeezed into cubes of rock wool and placed in the bottom of the first, raised tub.

(Rock wool is a grower's best friend. It's a highly absorptive material, similar to tightly spun cotton candy. The rock wool can retain massive amounts of water, but is soft enough to let roots penetrate as they grow.)

With the marijuana plants in place, a pump floods the table with water from the ground basin between one and six times a day to bring food and water to the roots. During the flooding periods, the rock wool retains enough water to keep the plant alive during the dry periods. This setup costs about $300.

For the Farm, Simon set up both ebb-and-flow and NFT systems. Each has its own benefit. Because rock wool retains so much water, if your system ever breaks down, your plants would be safe for a couple of days. If the NFT shuts down, it wouldn't forgive you: the pump goes, the roots dry out quickly, the plants die. However, with the ebb-and-flow, you have to buy new rock wool for each crop because the cubes can't be reused. With the NFT system, everything is reusable so your future costs are lower.

Simon had to build four wooden frames, one to hold each of the four systems that would be going into the room. These cost less than $10 each, factoring in the nails, screws, and wood. Everything in the room was already white, which would help reflect light back to the plants, but around the outside of each table, Simon also hung huge sheets of silver, reflective Mylar—kind of like giant, shiny sheets of aluminum foil, but not so moldable. This bounced even more light back onto the sun-ravenous plants and added only about $30 to the overall cost of the operation.

The final step was the exhaust system. First, Simon hung small, oscillating fans in each of the room's corners. At about $20 each, these small fans kept the air in the room circulating. Then Simon brought in a huge exhaust fan, worth about $150, to suck the air out of the room. The marijuana plants produce so much oxygen that there isn't enough carbon dioxide left in the grow room to keep the plants healthy. Plants need carbon dioxide to live, so Simon's exhaust fan sucked the high-oxygen air out of the room while a vent near the window replenished the room with fresh, carbon dioxide–rich air from outside. (Sometimes Simon brings in tanks of CO_2 and pumps it straight into the room but chose not to for the Farm.)

By the first week of February, the apartment was completely ready. It was a top-notch operation—efficient, sterile, and subtle. The final step was to bring in the marijuana plants.

You can grow marijuana from seeds or start off with cuttings from other healthy marijuana plants. These cuttings are called "clones" and are by far the preferred method of growing because you already know the sex. (Like all plants, there are male and female marijuana plants. Only the female plants flower and produce the valuable bud.)

The plants for the Farm were a set of clones that came from Simon's never-ending supply of "mother plants" he had stashed in friends' homes across the city. To make a clone, all Simon did was take clippings from these reliable marijuana producers, then put them in a root-building fertilizer solution until they developed a root system of their own. Once they had roots, they were ready to move. Simon brought about 70 new plants to the Farm, roughly 16 for each of the room's tables. There were all sorts of marijuana strains—Freezeland, Silver Pearl, Shiskaberry, Black Domino—all just inches high now but green with promise.

The plants were put under the spring light for the first two weeks. The most important thing for Simon was to check the water. There were two vital factors to monitor here: the nutrients and the pH balance of the water. Simon tested the water everyday to make sure the pH level in the water was constant and there was enough liquid fertilizer. The plants were on their way.

I made the drive up to Chelsea twice a week to visit the Farm, learning about the marijuana-growing process at Simon's side. By the end of the second week of February, the plants were spread out among the four tables, the summer/fall bulbs were in the light fixtures, and the lights were switched to a 12-hour cycle.

One day in late February, Simon had me over to the Farm to teach me how to thin and trim marijuana plants. The idea was to get as much light as possible to the buds. So that afternoon, Simon and I picked off thousands of the sickliest-looking marijuana leaves. As we worked, Simon explained to me in his Portuguese-French accent why he grew drugs.

"There are hundreds, thousands of ways to make money. This is good. I like the plants, they're like my children. I watch them grow, like babies. So what if it's against the law? The government can sell all the drugs it wants—alcohol, tobacco. What's wrong with pot? It makes people happy. I don't steal, I don't take welfare, I don't do anything. Who do I bother? Nobody."

He turned to me, his hands green from plant juice. "Is what I do so bad? Come on! Everybody loves marijuana. You know what I do sometimes? In the bar or in the taxi, when I'm about to pay, I take out my money in one hand and some pot in the other hand. I say, 'What do you want?' They always pick the pot. *Always.* I could have 50,000 watts going and still there wouldn't be enough pot. It's always dry. So, tell me, aren't I doing a good thing? I'm giving the people what they want."

I dropped a handful of leaves into a brown paper bag. But what about getting caught? I asked. What about your hash bust when you were a kid? Aren't you worried about doing time?

"You get caught, you get caught. I don't kill anybody. So maybe they'll put me in jail. I don't care. Hey, maybe if I ask nice they'll let me have 1000 watts in my cell."

Simon just wasn't ashamed of what he did. Hell, his parents in Portugal knew, and they just told him to be careful. When I tried to ask him another question about the risks, he just laughed and shook his head.

"You're too uptight. You need to relax, my friend. Smoke a joint."

Buds were already beginning to appear on the first table that day and the other three tables were close to blooming. By the following week, the first week of March, all the plants were decorated with rich, sticky buds that seemed to grow bigger before your eyes. Simon told me the tables would be ready to harvest by the last week of March.

The last time I had been at the Farm was the Sunday before the St. Patrick's Day bust. Simon was turning an empty room in the apartment into a drying room. He'd strung wires across the room to hang the marijuana on and had a couple of fans going to keep the air circulating. Steve showed up, and together they were going to cut and hang the first table. For an hour, they clipped branches off the plants and hung them upside down from the wires in the drying room. It was exciting to see the crop being harvested, but a little sad too. The table was once a sea of green and now it looked like a weed-whacker had gone at it.

"In a week, it'll dry," Simon told me.

I'd see him before that, I had promised, and walked out the door.

$ $ $

I get the phone message from Simon three days later. After I see the RCMP cop in the doorway, there's no question what's happened. Simon and the Farm had been busted.

The drive back from Chelsea is a blur. I keep on wondering if I could be caught up in all this. Had they followed my car? Had they been monitoring my visits? And what about the network? Through Simon, I'd met a lot of people, good people, in need. Middle-aged women, old men, retired government workers—all smoking to relieve the pain and sickness that life had cursed them with.

After getting back from Chelsea, I immediately go to see Steve at HMV. He's been trying to page Simon all day. He shakes his head glumly when I tell him about the police. He watches as kids in the store flip through the racks of CDs, deciding whether to buy Lauryn Hill or Korn.

"What about the other places?" Steve asks in a whisper.

"I only stopped at the Farm. I don't know about the others. I don't know about anything else," I say. "We'll have to wait until tomorrow."

The next morning, I sit in the back of Courtroom Six at the Ottawa courthouse. This is the bail court, the court where everybody who's been arrested and detained has to make their case for why they should be let out of custody until their trial. Usually, it is only the most heinous offenders—murderers, armed robbers, rapists—who are kept in. Most are let out on their own recognizance, meaning they agree to follow a set of strict rules with more criminal charges hanging over their head if they break them. Others are let out on bail, meaning they either have to put up money, or sign a surety saying they'll pay money if they breach the rules.

Simon is let out on his own recognizance. He agrees not to carry a cellphone or pager, to be at home between 11 p.m. and 6 a.m., and not to have anything to do with marijuana.

I buy him a coffee at the courthouse cafeteria after he is released. His eyes are rimmed with red, and grey-and-white stubble is splashed across his chin.

"I didn't have the most comfortable bed last night," Simon says with a wry smile.

Sipping a black coffee and watching the crowd warily, Simon runs down the situation. The RCMP busted two locations—Chelsea and Nepean. Somehow, the Hull and Ottawa sites were missed.

"I guess they don't do very good surveillance," shrugs Simon. "They could've followed me there easily. Those cops, they don't earn all their pay. I hope they don't get in trouble."

Simon finishes his coffee and gets up. He doesn't want to stay too long at the courthouse. He promises me he'll call soon.

The next day, the RCMP come to visit me. They'd seen my car at the Farm a few times, even trailing it to my girlfriend Paula's house once, and now they want to ask me a few questions. Thankfully, a lawyer friend of mine, Ken Hall, quickly chases them away. They weren't going to charge me, they just wanted me to make a statement against Simon. I'd rather have gone to jail.

Later that week, on Saturday morning, Simon and I meet at the Waffle House on Montreal Road to discuss the situation in full. I'd done the calculations: More than $35,000 worth of marijuana was destroyed. Another $15,000 in equipment was lost. And all the overhead costs—rent, hydro, materials and supplies—had been paid for without any return. That was another $5,000.

As he eats a waffle covered in sliced bananas, syrup and whipped cream, Simon is surprisingly upbeat for a man who'd just seen $55,000 slip through his fingers. If I had taken that loss, I'd have been devastated.

"It's not so bad. They didn't get it all," says Simon between bites. "There's still enough that people are going to get what they need."

And the money?

Simon points out that he'd grown more than 20 crops in the past two years alone.

"If that's the way they want to play, fine with me," Simon said. "I grow 20 crops for me, one crop for the government. What they hell? It's kind of like taxes."

But the real gleam in his eye is because he knows his beloved Co-Op isn't dead. The RCMP hadn't busted all his rooms, which means he has plenty of "mothers." From those mothers, he could clip a thousand more marijuana plants, and then a thousand more a few months after that. As for money, the doctors in Montreal have already come up with enough money to start another couple of operations. Simon had always boasted that all he needed was ten marijuana seeds in his pocket and he could be rich in a year. He had considerably more than that right now.

"What are they going to do to me? Put me in jail? How long can they do that for? Hey? You can't always win at this game. The police, they have to win sometimes too. So, let them win this one. And then it'll be my turn to win again."

I take out a $20 bill to pay for his waffle and my omelet. Simon shakes my hand and says he'll see me around. Then he presses a small plastic package into my hand. A little medical marijuana baggie, complete with a red cross and perhaps a half gram inside.

"A souvenir," he laughs, his smile as wide as I've ever seen it. He straightens his glasses, pats my shoulder, and leaves the restaurant.

$ $ $

Update: Medical Marijuana Users Get a (Very Small) Break

On Wednesday, June 11, 1999, Canada's health minister Alan Rock arrived in the House of Commons to make a historic announcement: Not only would the federal government start conducting clinical trials to determine the medical benefits of marijuana, but they would also grant two Canadian men the right to smoke marijuana without recrimination.

"This is about showing compassion to people, often dying, suffering from grave debilitating illness," Rock said.

The two men who can now smoke marijuana without fear of repercussion are Jim Wakeford and Jean-Charles Pariseau.

Wakeford, who lives in Toronto, had been fighting since 1997 to be exempted from prosecution for possessing and cultivating marijuana. The 54-year-old AIDS patient says the drug eases the side effects from his medication, such as nausea and loss of appetite. Similarly, Pariseau began a campaign to get legal marijuana in 1997 after the RCMP raided his Hull, Quebec, apartment and charged him with cultivating marijuana. Pariseau, 33, also suffering from AIDS, was growing and smoking his own marijuana on orders from his doctor.

"It's really like having a new life," Pariseau said after the minister's announcement. "I used to never know when the police would come in or if I would have some tomorrow. I was always worried because I need it."

The two men still have no legal way to get the drug and are forced to rely on the sympathy of underground medical marijuana networks. Under Rock's directive, Health Canada will now run trials to see if they can establish concrete medical benefits of the drug. If they do, the government will start a program to provide marijuana to people like Wakeford and Pariseau.

Rock did insist the new policy wasn't a step towards legalizing the drug — "no more than the use of heroin or morphine in hospitals is a step toward legalizing them."

The announcement by Rock followed similar decisions in the United States. According to the American group NORML (National Organization for the Reform of Marijuana Laws), between 1978 and 1996, 34 American states passed laws recognizing marijuana's therapeutic value and 23 of those laws remain in effect. Most recently, voters in Alaska, Oregon, Nevada, and Washington supported initiatives exempting patients who use marijuana under a physician's supervision from criminal penalties. But these states don't establish a legal supply for patients to obtain the drug. Just as Wakeford and Pariseau are forced to rely on underground networks, patients in these states still have to find their own source.

ROOTING AGAINST THE HABS: A SPORTS FAN KEEPS BOOK

Somehow, he just knew.

Even though the Pirates were down three games to one to the mighty Baltimore Orioles, Danny was sure they'd come back and win the World Series. He felt it. All you had to do was look at their line-up: Dave Parker in the outfield, Mike Easler on third, Willie Stargell on first, and if things got tense, Kent Tekulve in the bullpen to come in and close up. This was the "We Are Family" Pirates. This was destiny.

So when Billy Clayton started mouthing off about the bet, he was all over it. They were sitting in the cafeteria, eating peanut-butter-and-jam sandwiches their moms had packed for them and guzzling Coca-Cola. Danny was telling everybody at the table how sure he was that the Pirates would come back and win.

Billy smirked and told him, Hey, if you're so sure, why don't you put money where your mouth is? Danny bet Billy $5, straight up, that the Pirates would rally.

The World Series had opened in Baltimore that year and the teams split the first two games. When the Series shifted back to Pittsburgh, the O's won two straight, taking the commanding 3-1 lead. Then the Pirate magic kicked in. Stargell went on a tear and the pitching was hot, holding Baltimore to one run in Game 5 and shutting them out completely in Game 6. By Game 7, the Series was tied and the world was agreeing with Danny: This was destiny. The Pirates ended up winning Game 7 by a score of 4 to 1, with a two-run shot from Stargell in the ninth to seal the victory.

Danny had won his first bet. It was 1979 and he was just ten years old.

It took a while, but his next bet would be on the granddaddy of them all: the Super Bowl. Oakland versus Philadelphia, January 1981. For some reason, Danny was a Dick Vermeil fan. How many 11-year-olds even *knew* who coached the Eagles? But for that reason alone, Danny put his week's allowance down on Philadelphia. Unfortunately, Jim Plunkett had a huge game at quarterback for Oakland and Dick Vermeil's vaunted defensive schemes fell flat. The Raiders won 27-10 and Billy Clayton got his fiver back that day.

After that, betting seemed normal to Danny. He read the Vegas lines every morning in the newspaper along with the box scores and league standings. For fun, he'd make imaginary bets, keeping track of how he did in his math notebook. At school, if the other guys were talking about it he was betting on it. Small sums of course—five or ten dollars on the hockey playoffs, a Larry Holmes fight, even the Grey Cup.

A couple of years later, Danny was using his paper route money as a stake at neighbourhood poker games. By the time he reached high school, Danny was just known as a guy who bet. And bet well. He'd always devoured the sports pages and had subscriptions to both the *Sporting News* and *Sports Illustrated*. He knew who was injured, who was hot, and who was playing for a new contract.

After high school, Danny got a job waiting tables at an all-night deli downtown where his head for sports kept him in favour with the owner. Customers liked to talk sports and Danny could talk sports with the best of them. One his regulars when he worked the midnight shift was a guy named Jimmy, a fat Italian man with rings on every finger and a huge wad of cash. He was the best tipper in the deli and he loved to talk hockey.

Jimmy was from Laval, and seeing as Danny lived and died with the Montreal Canadiens, the two hit it off right away. It didn't take long for Danny to figure out the guy was booking—taking bets for a living. That just made Danny like Jimmy a little more and keep the Fat Man's coffee hotter and smoked meat sandwiches thicker.

They talked sports and they talked bets, night after night, Jimmy crammed into a red vinyl booth, Danny ignoring his other customers so the two could dissect that day's games. Danny was betting regular then, a couple of hundred a week from his tip money. He won more often than not, and loved nothing more than letting Jimmy know about his victories. Usually, the older man cackled away at Danny's stories of triumph, relishing the kid's excitement over such minor stakes.

But early one October morning in 1992, Jimmy arrived at the deli and wasn't so talkative. He drank his coffee but didn't touch the smoked meat. After some prodding, Jimmy finally admitted to Danny what had gone wrong. He'd taken a bath on that week's Monday night football game, Philadelphia and Dallas. The teams were undefeated going in and everybody wanted to bet on the big Monday nighter. Jimmy took a lot of Eagles action—too much as it turned out. They ended up destroying the Cowboys 31-7 and Jimmy was out tens of thousands. He'd taken a serious hit.

Danny shook his head as he listened. "Fuck, I could've *told* you Dallas was no good," Danny said. "Aikman's never been able to beat the Eagles. That was a gimme game."

Jimmy's eyes narrowed and he was about to tell the kid where to go. Danny ignored him and squeezed into the booth beside the Fat Man, explaining with all the cockiness and confidence of youth how he'd known all along that Philly was going to win that day. Eventually, the Fat Man smiled. He

Making Book: The Legalities

CRIMINAL CODE OF CANADA, SECTION 202

(1) Everyone commits an offence who

    (a) uses or knowingly allows a place under his control to be used for the purpose of recording or registering bets or selling a pool

    (d) records or registers bets or sells a pool

    (e) engages in book-making or pool selling, or in the business or occupation of betting

    (i) willfully and knowingly sends, transmits, delivers, or receives any message by radio, telegraph, telephone, mail, or express that conveys any information related to book-making, pool selling, betting or wagering

(2) Everyone who commits an offence under this section is guilty of an indictable offence and liable

    (a) for a first offence, to imprisonment for not more than two years

    (b) for a second offence, to imprisonment for not more than two years and not less than 14 days; and

    (c) for each subsequent offence, to imprisonment for not more than two years and not less than three months

started pushing his pickle around the plate with a fork as he listened to Danny carry on.

"Oh yeah?" said Jimmy. "You know so much, you're such a bright little kid, why dontcha do something about it? Huh? Why dontcha?"

"Like what? Go to Vegas?"

"Don't be stupid," answered the Fat Man. "Why dontcha come work for me?"

Danny needed about two seconds to make that decision. He already loved to bet and he liked Jimmy. Then there was the money. The Fat Man carried around a wad of twenties the size of a baseball. Who wouldn't want a piece of that?

"What do you want me to do?" asked Danny.

Jimmy speared the pickle and took a bite.

"We'll work something out, kid."

$ $ $

It was like an apprenticeship. Danny was 23 years old and about to receive an Ivy League education in betting. After a couple of more late-night dinners at the deli, Danny and the Fat Man came to an arrangement: Danny would act as an agent, bringing in bets, handling some action for Jimmy. He didn't have to worry about money—Jimmy would back every bet. He did need to get out there and find the players and collect the winnings. In return, Danny would get a choice weekly commission.

Danny was ready to get to work when that year's NFL playoffs rolled around a couple months later. It couldn't have been a more auspicious beginning. The Houston Oilers versus the Buffalo Bills was the hot game that week and Danny took in a lot of action on the Oilers. Houston had killed the Bills the last time they'd played and for the playoff game, both the Bills quarterback, Jim Kelly, and one of their top linebackers, Cornelius Bennett, were injured. Nobody was betting Buffalo.

Sure enough, on game day, Houston was leading 35-3 in the third quarter. Then the backup QB, Frank Reich, became a miracle worker. The Bills poured it on and stormed back, tying the game 38-38 and then winning it on a Steve Christie field goal in overtime. It was the biggest comeback in NFL history. It also made Danny and the Fat Man some nice extra money. A comeback like that on his first weekend in business—it was like God telling Danny he'd found his calling.

After the nervousness of the first weekend and the incredible Bills game, Danny slipped into a good rhythm. He knew dozens of guys who liked to bet, so he just lined them up with Jimmy, took the bets, and called them in. After a while, he started bringing in new money too. People he served, guys he played pick-up hockey with, even the owner of the deli started making a bet or two through Danny.

"It's easy, it's like a fish on a line," Danny'd explain. "You hook'em and reel'em in, just like Jimmy did to me.

"Say you're at a bar, watching a game. You and the guy next to you start talking, and he keeps on checking the scores. He pulls out a Pro-Line ticket, and you ask, 'How'd you do?' And he'd say something like, 'Ah, I lost. Only got five out of six.' You just tell him, 'Pro-Line is for suckers. You should never have to bet more than one game unless you want to.'"

That was always enough to get a betting conversation started. And Danny found that, more often than not, the guy was interested. If he already bet on Pro-Line, he was half-way hooked. Players liked betting through a bookie more than they did a government lottery; they liked telling their co-workers and friends they bet with a bookie and the odds were a hell of a lot better than anything the government could offer.

To Danny, the fact that the government-run sports lottery made you bet three games minimum was straight-out robbery. It's simple odds: If you bet one game, you have a one-in-two chance of winning. If you have to bet three games, all the possible scenarios mean your odds drop to one in eight—plain robbery.

"What we're doing might be illegal," Danny'd say, "but what the government's doing, that's amoral."

After six months of working for Jimmy the Fat Man, Danny knew he could go out on his own. He had a good group of clients he'd built up over the past half-year and thanks to Jimmy, he knew booking inside out.

$ $ $

There were two ways a bookie made money: off the juice and when a player lost his bets.

The juice was a commission paid to the bookie for handling the action. It was usually 10 per cent, or "a dime on" as it's called, and it was easy money. The juice worked like a penalty. A player calls in and bets $100 on the Dallas Cowboys to win a Monday night game against the New York Giants. If the Cowboys win, Danny owes the player $100. But if the Cowboys lose, the player owes Danny $110—the $100 plus the 10 per cent juice. It's simply the cost of doing business, and all gamblers pay it without question.

In an ideal world, a bookie could just balance the books and live off the juice. Say on that one Dallas game, you have 20 players betting $100 on the

Cowboys to win and another 20 players betting $100 on the Giants to win. No matter what happens that night, Danny is going to owe $2,000 but collect $2,200 because the losers have to pay the 10 per cent juice. That's $200 in Danny's pocket for simply transferring the money between the losers and the winners. When the action gets serious and you start taking bets in the $5,000 range, the juice becomes worthwhile.

The way to live off the juice, though, is to even up your books: Always have the same amount of money riding on Team A as you do on Team B. If you have $10,000 on the Cowboys and $10,000 on the Giants, you sleep well that night knowing you've got $1,000 in your pocket with no risk to you. But if you get $50,000 worth of bets on the Cowboys and only $10,000 worth of bets on the Giants, you're out on a limb. You're either up $45,000 or down $39,000 at the end of the night, depending who wins. No quicker route to the poorhouse or an ulcer.

There are two ways to even your books. The first is through the lines. When the Vegas line comes out at the beginning of the week, it might have Dallas as a seven-point favourite. That means if a player bets on Dallas, the Cowboys have to beat the Giants by at least eight points for them to win their money. Likewise, if you bet on the Giants and they lose 24-20 to the Cowboys, you still get paid because the seven-point spread means as long as they lose by six points or less, the bet is good. (If the Cowboys win by seven exactly, nobody wins.)

So, if a bookie notices the money starting to pile up on Dallas, he'll start to move the line to bring in more bets on the Giants. Instead of a seven-point spread, he'll offer a nine-and-a-half-point spread. That makes it a little bit

---

Vegas Line Bet Example

Odds: Team A to win by 7-point spread:

FINAL SCORES

Team A	Team B	Betting Result
24	20	If you bet on A, you lose; if you bet on B, you win
28	20	If you bet on A, you win; if you bet on B, you lose
20	24	If you bet on A, you lose; if you bet on B, you win
27	20	Even money; nobody pays anything.

harder for the Cowboys to cover—they'd have to beat the Giants by ten points for someone betting Dallas to make money—so people start putting money on the Giants now. Slowly, your book evens out.

The second way for a book to even up his bets is to push some of the action off to another bookie. It's a small gambling community; the books all know each other and some actually try to help each other out. If Danny's got $50,000 on the Cowboys and $10,000 on the Giants, he starts calling around to other books. Likely, he'll find one who has more money riding on the Giants than the Cowboys. So, Danny would "push" $20,000 or $30,000 worth of his customers' bets to another bookie. That way, neither of them is exposed to as big a risk and they still make their money off the juice.

Of course, the world isn't perfect and you can rarely completely balance your books, but in the end that doesn't matter too much because the juice gives the bookie a 10 per cent cushion to protect himself. If Danny had $50,000 on the Cowboys and only $45,000 on the Giants and the Cowboys won, he'd only be out $500 because he'd collect $4,500 in juice off the losers. The juice kept the books in business.

The other way bookies make money is when gamblers lose "sucker bets." Straight-up bets on football and basketball games pay one-to-one—you bet a dollar, you win a dollar. But gamblers like long shots. They like to try and make a bit more money off you by betting more than one game at once. These are the sucker bets.

Danny offered these parlays on both football and basketball games. In this case, players would bet two, three, or four games at once, with all of them having to come in for the gambler to win. The payoff was higher if the player won—Danny paid out $2.65 on the dollar for two games, $5.95 on the dollar for three games and $10 on the dollar for four games. That meant if you put down $1,000 and picked three NFL games correctly, you'd get $5,950—a major score.

But Danny loved taking these bets because they were easy money, since the odds were so good they wouldn't come in. Let some guy bet $1,000 on both the Cowboys beating the Giants and the Miami Dolphins beating the Kansas City Chiefs. Sure, if both the Cowboys and Dolphins win and beat the point spread, you have to pay out more—$2,650 instead of $1,000—but the odds are all in the book's favour.

First you have to assume that the bookmakers in Vegas are on the money—and they usually are. That means, they've come up with point spreads on the two games that pretty much even out the games—say the Cowboys have to win by seven to cover and the Dolphins have to win by

Sucker Bets

Betting on two games, your chances of winning are only 1 in 4

Example: You bet A to beat B, and C to beat D; there are four possible outcomes (not including cases where the point spread
is equalled), only one of which will result in a winning bet:

A beats B, C beats D	You win!
A beats B, C loses to D	You lose!
A loses to B, C beats D	You lose!
A loses to B, C loses to D	You lose!

two—so it's a toss-up which team wins. In that scenario, there are four possible combinations: Cowboys and Dolphins win, Cowboys and Chiefs win, Giants and Dolphins win, and Giants and Chiefs win. The chances of the guy pulling off his Cowboys and Dolphins bet is only one in four. That makes the odds 75-25 in Danny's favour. All you had to do was the math. You take four bets like that, at $1,000 each, the law of averages says that only one of them is coming in. That means for every four bets Danny takes, he's going to collect $3,300—three times $1,000 plus the 10 per cent juice from the losers. He only has to pay out $2,650 to the one winner, so it's a profit of $650.

These bets are a bit riskier because you can't insulate yourself by evening your book like you can with straight-up bets. But the odds are that the gambler is going to lose three times out of four, which makes the bookie some good money. Of course, a bookie might be on the hook for a bigger payoff once in a while, but unless he's the unluckiest son of a bitch around, he's usually going to make money.

Danny only offered the parlays on NBA and NFL games because the bets on baseball and hockey work a bit differently. Both basketball and football are governed by point spreads. If the best team in the NFL plays the worst team in the NFL, the best would probably be favoured by at least 14 points. That means if you bet on the favourite, the favourite has to win by 15 points or more for you to get your money. The same point spreads worked with basketball, with the best teams being favoured by 10 or 15 points over the worst teams. (In college basketball and football, where there is more disparity, the point spreads are absurd. It's not unusual to see a major college like Florida State favoured by 40 or 50 points over a small school.)

In baseball and hockey, the games are different. There aren't enough

"Money Lines" Bet Example

BOB—Bets on the favourite: $220 to win $100
RAY—Bets on the underdog: $100 to win $180

Winner?	Bookie Pays	Loser Pays Losing Bet + 10% Juice	Bookie Earns
Favourite	$100 to Bob	$110 from Ray	$10
Underdog	$180 to Ray	$242 from Bob	$62
Tie	nothing	nothing	nothing

points—goals and runs, actually—scored in either hockey or baseball to make a point spread viable. So bookies usually take bets on baseball and hockey using money lines.

If one of the top baseball teams, like the New York Yankees, was going to play one of the worst teams, like the Montreal Expos, the Yanks would be heavily favoured. But instead of a run spread—say, New York has to beat the 'Spos by four runs to win the bet—bookies offer money lines based on the magical $100 figure. In this case, it'd be something like 220-180. If you bet on the favoured Yankees, you have to bet $220 to win $100. If you bet on the underdog Expos, you bet $100 to win $180. A bookie makes his money on those bets off the 10 per cent juice and the difference in payoffs. If you get one bet on the Yankees and one on the Expos, and Montreal pulls off the upset, the bookie collects $242 from the loser ($220 plus the ten per cent juice) and pays out $180 to the winner—a quick $62 profit.

Bookies never offer parlays on money lines because it would be easier for the player. Without the spread to even out the teams, you could pick three baseball games where Roger Clemens, Greg Maddux and Randy Johnson were pitching against some minor-league rejects and have a pretty good shot at landing your bet. Those odds wouldn't be in the book's favour, so that offer wouldn't be on the table.

$ $ $

It took a couple of weeks working under Jimmy for Danny to soak all this in, but he loved math and sports so it was a labour of love. It was a hell of a lot more fun than Grade 12 calculus class.

By the time the 1993 NFL season started, he was ready to go out on his own. Jimmy had no problem with Danny's decision. In fact, he was even a little bit proud, like a father watching his son start his first job. Danny still worked at the deli—it was a great way to pick up new clients and the owner was quickly becoming his best customer—and the Fat Man still ate his smoked meat and drank his coffee. However, now when they talked, they talked about their action, what customers were paying and which ones weren't, who was on a winning streak and who was just chasing their money.

Because he'd built up a following while apprenticing for the Fat Man, Danny had no shortage of customers at the beginning. What he did need, though, was a partner. Danny was a fair-sized guy, about 5 feet 11, and he had muscles—he'd been working out since he was 16. The problem was, he was just too good looking. He had a movie-star face. Naturally dark skin, brilliant blue eyes, sandy-blond hair, strong features. Girls went crazy over him. Guys, well, sometimes guys didn't take him too seriously.

What he needed was somebody to help with the phones and help collect the debts. Not necessarily a heavy, but a least somebody heavier. He chose one of his old drinking buddies from high school, Pete, a big guy with a tough face. He'd played football at university, tight end, so he had the strength. And he also had the disposition. There was something menacing in his eyes. Pete was the kind of man who stopped fights in bars just by standing up. Seeing as he loved sports and loved to bet, he was a good sidekick to have.

Between the tips he was earning at the deli and the commissions he'd earned off Jimmy the Fat Man, Danny had a nice little roll built up. If he cleaned out all his accounts, he could come up with $25,000. That was more than enough to get started. Realistically, unless there was trouble, the odds said he wouldn't be paying out anything that big for a while. The $25,000 would cover him if he suffered a losing week or two before the odds kicked in and his players started losing.

The players didn't notice the difference at first. Like always, Danny still took their bets. And like always, Danny always picked up and dropped off the money on Fridays. The only time they'd notice the difference would be if the debt settlement wasn't quite so amicable. Then, instead of Jimmy's boys paying them a visit, it would be Danny and Pete.

Those first weeks were a blur for Danny. He couldn't sleep. All he did was watch the sports ticker on CNN at night, his mind running a hundred different odds at once. He'd get up at 4 a.m. and run through his ledger of bets, calculating how much he stood to earn—or lose—on the week.

Like all bookies, Danny worked his accounts weekly, with Friday being pay-out day. For regular players and seasoned bookies, there was no point in settling accounts after every bet. Too much headache and hassle. A player could owe the bookie $2,000 on Sunday after losing a bunch of NFL games, make $1,000 back on baseball on Tuesday and then win another $500 Thursday. When Friday comes around, the bettor can settle his $500 debt. There was no point in passing the money back and forth every day.

Of course, in that same scenario, the player doesn't necessarily have to pay off at the end of the week. Like credit card companies, bookies give their customers a limit. If your limit is $5,000, you can carry a $3,000 debt for a couple of weeks. If you lose big and go down $7,500, you have to pay at least $2,500 on Friday to get below your limit.

The credit limits protect both the player and the bookie. A player knows he can't go down too much and the bookie knows he'll be able to collect. Without a limit, a guy could just chase his money forever. A gambler who is down, their first instinct is to bet more to try and get back up again. It can get ridiculous, with a guy owing fifty, sixty even a hundred thousand. Most guys can't pay that kind of money, so there's no point in a bookie letting them bet that kind of action; if the book wins, he won't see the return. The limit keeps the bettor in the game and the book at least making money off the guy.

At the end of Danny's third week, he sat down and added up the numbers. He was astounded: He'd taken more than $400,000 in bets in one week. He shook his head. *Impossible*, he thought. He added up the numbers and they were right. That's when he realized that it was all fake. Sure, he might have taken bets for all the money, but it was an illusion.

"Here's how it works," he explained. "On a Saturday morning, you might get a call from a bartender. He bets $100 on the Notre Dame game at one o'clock. He wins, and he lets it ride on another college game at four. He wins again and now he's up $400. He thinks 'What the hell,' and he bets it again on the NFL games on Sunday. He wins the one o'clock, he wins the four, he wins the Sunday night game. He's up $3,200 now. He lets it ride on the Monday nighter and wins.

Government Action

Bookies live off the mere crumbs of the gambling industry. By far, the majority of wagering in Canada is done through government-run operations like casinos, lotteries, sports betting and video lottery terminals. And while a bookie is lucky to make $100,000 in a year, the government is close to making $10,000,000,000 a year off of its "players."

"Now he's up six-and-a-half and feels good. So that Tuesday, he lets it ride again on a hockey game. And the thing is, he tells his buddy he's got $13,000 riding on the game. That's bullshit. All he ever was on the line for was the $100. Sure, if he wins, he's up $13,000, but it's a fake number."

Likewise, a guy might place ten $500 bets with Danny in a week. He wins six, loses four. Danny ends up paying out a just $800—the player won $3,000 and lost $2,000 plus the $200 juice on the losses. The books show that Danny handled $5,000 worth of action off this guy. There was no way Danny would ever have been on the hook for the $5,000. Nobody can pick ten winners in a week. The odds are impossible.

But if the high numbers were fake, the money Danny earned was definitely not. In his first year, he was pulling in a couple thousand a week, no problem. On big weeks, he might take home $20,000. Of course, the next week, he might pay out $15,000, but the law of averages was working.

There was no question he liked the money. He drove a nice car, bought $200 shirts, took girls out and treated them right. When his best friend couldn't get a student loan, it was nice to be able to lend him $10,000. And he liked the buzz. People were quickly finding out who he was.

"You walk into a bar, and people *know*. You hear the whispering. They know who you are. You can hear them, leaning over to their friends, saying, 'Look. See that guy? He handles action.'"

It was a good life for Danny. Not that there wasn't a downside, though. He'd be out at a restaurant with a girl, going full out, having a great meal, and still he couldn't keep his head off the games. He'd sneak off every 30 minutes to check the scores on the phone line, ruining the meal. On big nights, he couldn't concentrate on anything but the games.

Then there were the loyalties. For years Danny had loved the Montreal Canadiens. Les Habitants were part of his life. He had their home and away jerseys. He still had shoeboxes filled with hockey cards and he could recite the lineups of the 1976 to 1979 Stanley Cup teams in his sleep. His beautiful golden retriever was even named Rocket after the great Maurice Richard.

It happened out of the blue. He was in the living room with his ledger book, running down the night's bets, doing the quick math to determine how different results would affect his bottom line. When he looked up, the Canadiens-Penguins highlights were being shown. The Penguins were up 5-1 in the third period. And he was happy. He was actually happy his beloved Habs were losing because it meant an extra $14,000 for him. He was no longer a sports fan. He was a businessman.

That wasn't all that bothered Danny. He knew some of the players betting with him couldn't afford it. He knew they had problems, serious addictions. Money that should be going to their mortgage or their kid's university tuition was going to him.

All Danny told himself was that if these guys didn't bet through him, they'd bet somewhere else. And that was the truth. There were dozens of bookies in town, there were the government-run sports lotteries, there was the off-shore telephone betting, there were the casinos. Gambling was a part of life. He'd once heard somebody say that if wasn't for gambling, there'd be seven people watching football on Sundays. That was an exaggeration in Danny's mind, but not much of one.

Of course, what he was doing was illegal. He could face jail time, Danny knew that. But the reality was, police didn't care about bookies. Once, the local cops had spent more than $1 million on an undercover investigation to try and crack down on the illegal books. They ended up making more than 20 arrests. Not one person ended up spending a day in jail. A couple of the big guys got nailed with probation and $25,000 fines, but almost everybody else just had to pay a grand or two and walked away. Danny knew another big book in Toronto who went down in 1994. The cops popped him doing $50 million in action a year. What he'd get? A measly $100,000 fine.

The judges and lawyers knew what Danny knew: Society just wasn't that concerned about bookies, at least not concerned enough to see precious tax money spent keeping them in jail.

The worst part of the job was collecting debts. Ideally, the players would show up at your doorstep Friday morning with cash in their hand. But life wasn't ideal.

There were guys who simply couldn't pay, and as long as they weren't in to Danny too much, that was fine. He'd work out a payment plan, promise the guy once he got it paid off he could bet again, be very cordial about it. Of course, that was a lie. Once Danny got his money, the player was cut off and he let the other books in town know that this guy was chasing his money now and not good for any of it. But at least it was civil.

The problems came when a player did have the money, but just didn't want to pay. Somebody would collect $2,000 off Danny one week and not be able to pay the $1,500 he owed two weeks later. That pissed him off.

"You have to a be a good actor. I got good at it," Danny said.

He and Pete would arrive at the house or apartment and make it very clear they expected their money. *Tomorrow*. Pete, if necessary, would threaten violence. They would return the next day for their money. If the client didn't have it, something would be broken—not a bone, but a television, a framed picture, an antique vase. Preferably something the wife would notice. The message was clear: Make arrangements by tomorrow or the damage would be physical, not material.

While they didn't always get their money the next day, they always got at least a down payment and a promise to pay the rest very soon. There hadn't been any real violence yet. They were adults after all and this was definitely not a Robert DeNiro movie.

By the end of his first year in business, Danny had built himself a nice little reputation. He always paid his debts and he never screwed around. In return, he had mostly good customers. Real gamblers. The worst thing for a bookie was the guy who was in it for the money, the guy who always quit when he was ahead.

There was one player he had, if he was down, he'd bet like a demon all week to get back even by Friday. On the other hand, if the player was up a couple of thousand after the weekend action, he'd disappear until Friday so he could collect. Danny hated it when they ran away and hid like that, but there was nothing to be done about it.

For Danny, the best clients were the players who made the same bets all the time, win or lose, no matter where they stood. A couple of games a night, every night, for these guys. They did it for the thrill of it, for the need of it. This was Danny's bread and butter.

He made his regular money on hockey. He worked in Canada after all, and guys couldn't seem to bet enough on the sport. But the real fun was NFL Sundays. That was the big deal all over North America and that was the day serious money was won or lost. On Sunday mornings in the fall and early winter there'd be a buzz in the air. Danny and Peter would have four phones going to take the bets. They started coming in heavy at about 9 a.m., once the guys had read their morning papers for last-minute injury updates and digested the betting columns. There was another flurry just after the television pregame shows finished at 1 p.m.

The busiest days of all were Sundays in early October. You had the NFL, you had the baseball playoffs, and you had the start of the hockey season. You could have 25 big games that day, games that bettors had serious interest in. The phone didn't stop ringing all day.

The most fantastic day was the Super Bowl. It was the day everybody bet, from the guy pumping gas at the Esso to the high-paid software engineer to Danny's own mother. Vegas estimates $4-billion is wagered each year on that one single day. *Four billion*. The number is staggering, but believable. Danny made the day fun. He let every bet ride, from who'd win the coin toss to who'd score the first touchdown. It was the one day that the world seemed to publicly celebrate gambling.

$ $ $

By Super Bowl XXIX in 1995, Danny had been in the business for two years. He was established now, taking more action than his old mentor Jimmy the Fat Man. That year, he made the most money he'd ever earned—more than $240,000.

Everything was going right for him. His clients were losing far more often than they won. And Danny was betting upwards of $2,000 a week himself now and winning far more than he lost. To reward himself, he put a $5,000 bet on the 49ers in the Super Bowl. They ended up blowing out the San Diego Chargers. A perfect ending.

At that point, everything looked good. Most books can work a lifetime. There are always enough gamblers, the police aren't a big concern, and the work, though stressful, is lucrative. Danny didn't think once of getting out.

But by the time the next Super Bowl rolled around in 1996, Danny's game had started to falter. His profits were down and his own gambling losses were up. He'd fallen into the easiest trap of them all: He had started to buy his own sales pitch. Like the coke dealer who ends up putting his profits up his nose, Danny had started making a few too many bets of his own.

Just like back in grade school, when his gut had told him the Pirates would win, Danny always trusted his instinct when it came to sports. Part of him always thought he had a genuine sixth sense that gave him an advantage over everybody else. His first three years in the booking business, his instincts had been generally right. He'd made a lot of money betting on the side, and even if he lost a bundle now and again, he didn't feel it because the profits from the book were so good.

What he didn't realize was that he was going to have a run of bad luck. All of 1996, his instinct was a little off, like the NBA player who suddenly can't make a free throw for the life of him, or the shortstop who out of the blue can't make the throw to first any more. He was making personal bets more than ever, but he was losing far more often than he was winning. He was paying those gambling losses out of his booking profits and the bottom line was really starting to suffer. At the end of that year, he estimated he'd cleared only $130,000. Well, Danny told himself, that's as bad as it gets.

The thing is, it got worse. By the time the Packers won the Super Bowl in January 1997, he was losing regularly on his bets with other bookies, and his customers were winning regularly enough off him that he couldn't cushion the losses. By summer 1997, he was actually starting to chase his own money. To compound the problem, instead of concentrating on booking, he started concentrating on betting. He stopped looking for new customers and started turning off his pager and cellphone so he could focus on the games he had money riding on. All of a sudden he was more of a player than a book.

By the time the NFL season started again in the fall of 1997, Danny knew he was done. He was betting every day and it wasn't good betting. He no longer took the best game on the board, he took the televised game so at least he could watch his money disappear live on TV.

Then there was that feeling when he won. It used to be euphoria. Now it was just relief that he hadn't lost. He'd once had dozens of big players betting with him, but one by one they had moved on to more reliable books. The first couple weeks of the NFL season he tried to keep it going, but it was no use. He was done.

Five years after Jimmy the Fat Man had taken him under his wing, Danny was out of business, taken down by the same thing that makes booking such a good business to begin with: the insatiable urge to bet.

$ $ $

It's late now. Danny's been talking for almost six straight hours. He's been through a couple of pints and still his throat is raw.

"I need a drink. Water," he says, turning to search out the waitress.

It's after midnight and the talk and laughter in the bar are loud now, much louder than they'd seemed when Danny was talking. Frowning, he stares after the waitress.

"I don't know. What do I have now? I'm not sure."

It's been more than a year-and-a-half since he took his last bet. He earns good money now as a waiter, turning his Hollywood looks into big tips. He hasn't put any money on a game for more than a year.

"When it's said and done, I don't know. Am I better for it?" He shrugs again. "The sucker always says, 'If I stay at the poker table long enough, I'm going to win my money.' The smart player says, 'If I stay at the poker table long enough, I'm going to lose my money.' I stayed at the table too long."

He's not yet 30, but he's got the countenance of a veteran, one of those old guys who has seen so much that by the time he gets home from the war, all he needs is a front porch, a newspaper and a quart of beer to make him happy. For Danny, he doesn't know exactly what he wants now, other than to relax.

He spends time with his daughter. He plans to get married to the woman he loves. He enjoys drinking a cold beer with old friends.

"I don't miss it. Sure, I liked it, I liked the feeling. But that's gone now," he says. "I don't even feel the urge to bet, not really anyway."

The waitress brings his water and he drinks it down straight. She turns to leave but Danny catches her arm and orders a fresh pint of beer.

"You know what?" he says, admiring the waitress's legs as she walks off, "I can watch the Habs again. That's the best part. They're going to put it together soon, for a whole season, you know they are. I'll be there for the Stanley Cup, I'll be there centre ice. And I'll be cheering."

ON THE BRINK:
A THIEF LOOKS FOR A JOB

Ian is trying hard to be a straight john, but sometimes it stings him to be just another guy.

Like the other day. A movie was being shot outside of town, so he and his buddies drove out to be extras. A bunch of actors were there, some Ian even recognized from TV, and Ian was loving it. Sure, he was getting paid minimum wage, but he was actually *getting paid* to run around in the snow dressed up like an American soldier. It was a blast!

But there he was, lounging around in the trailer, drinking hot chocolate, waiting for another of his scenes to start. Beside him was one of the movie's supporting actors. Together they watched through the window as another group of extras, British soldiers this time, marched across the field for the cameras.

"So this one guy, he falls down," Ian says, his face contorting with anger as he tells the story to his friend Paul. "They were marching across the field, shoulder to shoulder, in formation, and his shoe gets stuck in the snow and comes off. So he goes after it. But when he turns around, he gets trampled by the other guys coming up behind him. Trampled. Real idiot. Anyway, the guy next to me, he must have been making some money, I don't know how much, but some good money, he was one of the main actors, he goes: 'Look at those idiots, running around like that in the field for minimum wage. Can you believe that? Who would do that?'

"I look back at him and I don't say anything, but I feel like a vagrant. *A vagrant.* I feel like saying, 'Buddy, do you know who I am? Do you know the moves I've pulled?' I know it shouldn't, but it gets to me. It really does."

Ian is telling the story to his friend Paul as they sit and drink beer and watch football. It's Saturday and the NFL playoffs are on. Denver is kicking the shit out of Miami in the third quarter.

Paul is definitely a straight john. He's never pulled a move of any kind, ever. He's proud of the fact that every dollar he's ever earned was earned honestly.

Ian, Ian is most definitely not a straight john. He's pulled more moves than Bobby Fischer and as a result has done his share of time in jail. Ian's back out now, trying to keep it straight and legal, trying to be a straight john like Paul. But it was hard.

They drink their beers in silence for a while, Paul wanting to let Ian cool down a bit. On the big-screen TV, Elway throws for another touchdown to put the Broncos up 31-3. This suits Ian just fine. He has $2,000 down on Denver to win.

"Look," Paul finally says. "You're young. You've never actually had to rough it. What—you were, like, fifteen when you started? How much money were you making at fifteen? A couple hundred a week. Most kids have, what—thirty bucks a week? Hell, I was packing groceries back then, twenty hours a week, and making maybe, *maybe* a hundred dollars a week. You had tons of money then, you never had to rough it. And you haven't had to rough it since, not once in the past ten years, except when you were in jail. So now, now you have to rough it a bit. Big deal. You can handle it."

"Yeah, I guess," says Ian, smiling a little now at the memory of his glory days.

Postage Paid

By far, one of the most successful break-and-enter rings in the history of Canada was the Champagne Gang. Over a six-year period, four young men—Kevin Grandmaison, Yves Belanger, Marc Flamini and Tyler Wilson—executed more than 200 rooftop break-and-enters at pharmacies, gorcery stores and postal outlets across the country. It is estimated they netted between $4-  and $6-million on their spree and astoundingly, a good chunk of that money was netted from the simple postage stamp.

Whenver they hit a store, the foursome always made sure to get the stamps. It may not sound consequential, but a 10-pack of first class stamps is smaller than a bill and at that time was worth $4.30. When you start taking stamps by the armload—tens of thousands at a time—it adds up quick. The gang would sell the stamps to chains of convenience stores at 50 cents on the dollar, and from each of their break-and-enters they could usually count on walking away with $5,000 to $10,000 in stamps, along with the contents of the safe.

"I was working at fifteen, I was pulling some moves, but I never made any real money until I was sixteen, seventeen. Back then I had money and everybody knew it. All my friends, I'd buy them lunch, I'd buy their soups, I'd buy them whatever. No word of a lie, they all knew I had money, lots of it."

"Exactly," says Paul, rallying now. "That's what I'm saying. From then on, from that point on, you never had to rough it once. You were never a vagrant. You never had to start at the bottom. Now you have to start at the bottom."

Ian nods and takes another tug on his beer. Outside, a diesel truck rumbles by and he watches out the window as the black exhaust fumes disappear into the January air.

"You know, it's funny," Ian says. "There I was, just a couple of years ago, grabbing $48,000 just like that, thinking nothing about it, grabbing it whenever I wanted. And I remember before when I was a kid, when I was sixteen or seventeen, I heard about a guy pulling $30,000 and I used to say, 'Wow, imagine that! *Imagine* that kind of money.' But I had it, I had it and it was nothing. Now I'm thinking, what if, what if I pulled a box with one-fifty? What if? You know, $150,000 doesn't even seem that crazy to me now. It's funny, you know, the way these things happen."

Paul shakes his head. He had no answer for that one. Everyone's Achilles' heel was escalating expectations. Paul remembered when he started university, he thought if he could make $30,000 a year, he'd be the happiest guy in the

Break and Enter: The Legalities

CRIMINAL CODE OF CANADA, SECTION 348

(1) Every one who

    (a) breaks and enters a place with intent to commit an indictable offence therein or

    (b) breaks and enters a place and commits and indictable offence therein is guilty of an indictable offence and liable

        (i) to imprisonment for life, if the offence is committed in relation to a dwelling house or

        (ii) to imprisonment for a term not exceeding fourteen years, if the offence is committed in relation to a place other than a dwelling house.

world. Now he was making fifty-five and was scheming to get up to seventy. Nobody was ever happy with what they had. Why should Ian be any different?

Ian throws back the rest of his beer and stubs his cigarette out in Paul's prized Cuban ashtray. He stands up, tugging his leather jacket straight. Ian is six feet two inches and keeps his curly blond hair cropped tight to his skull. He has the tough looks of a hockey goon, a guy whose face has taken a couple of beatings but who is still handsome enough to get the girls. He's styling today too, with a cobalt blue shirt, black cords, black, loosely tied ankle-high Doc Martens and a black leather jacket. He checks the time on a wristwatch that cost more than Paul earns in a month.

"So, we're still on for tomorrow?"

Paul has to suppress a laugh. "If you're still up for it, we're on. Absolutely."

Ian had dropped by to see if Paul would help him with his resumé. He wants to try and get a straight job, to do things legitimately. But things didn't look good for Ian, that's all Paul could say. Talking about pulling a safe job for $150,000—even if it was just talk, that's not a good way to start off on a new career path. Ian is definitely on the brink.

"Yeah, Paulie, for sure," says Ian. "I'll drop by about ten."

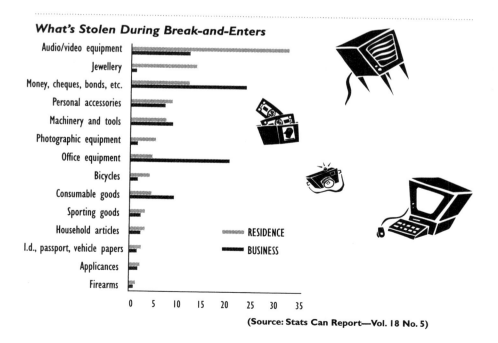

What's Stolen During Break-and-Enters

(Source: Stats Can Report—Vol. 18 No. 5)

Paul says goodbye and watches Ian slip out the front door and cross the street to where his Jeep is parked. He stands there long after Ian has driven off, long after the January wind has numbed his skin. Finally, he turns and gets another bottle of Canadian from the fridge. Denver was threatening to score again.

$ $ $

Ian and Paul had been friends for almost 20 years. They'd grown up together in Ottawa's east end, their parents living on the same block in the suburb of Orleans. As kids they'd played hockey and baseball together, gone to the same kindergarten and grade school, and slept over at each other's houses on weekends. There was a whole gang of them from the neighbourhood like Ian and Paul, kids who hung out, rode their bikes and played sports.

Then, when the boys were nine, Ian's dad kind of took off. Ian didn't talk about it much, but for a while he started staying at Paul's house almost every night. After a while, Ian's mom couldn't afford the rent for the townhouse in Orleans any more, so she and Ian moved to a two-bedroom apartment closer to downtown.

The two boys still played on the same baseball team, but Ian stopped hanging around the Orleans kids and picked up with some new friends from around his building. By the time they reached high school in the fall of 1986, Ian was a completely different guy. He had an air of toughness about him he didn't have before and to Paul's amazement, he'd started drinking in Grade 8.

Paul and he had little in common by then, but for old time's sake they still said hi, talked about Gary Carter and the Expos, and of course, girls, although Ian always had a lot more of them around him than Paul ever did.

....

Residential B & E Risk in Industrialized Countries
(Results of 1996 International Crime Victimization Survey)

England & Wales	6.1%
Canada	5.3
Netherlands	5.1
USA	4.9
France	3.9
Scotland	3.6
Northern Ireland	2.5

(Source: Quoted in Statistics Canada, Catalogue no. 85-002-XPE, Vol. 18, No. 5, p. 3)

They might have drifted completely apart, except for what happened at the end of Grade 9.

Paul was still awkward, had the start of a bad acne problem and was probably a bit too smart for his own good. A couple of guys from Grade 11, Jason Fitch and Terry Drummond, had been picking on him, making him pay "protection" out of the money he earned at the grocery store.

One time in April, Jason and Terry were pushing Paul around in the high school parking lot at lunch hour, asking where their $20 was. Paul was crying, he couldn't help himself. He'd been giving them $20 a week for months and that day he didn't have any money on him. He'd been saving since Christmas and had spent all his money buying an Apple computer. His next paycheque wasn't for another week.

Paul was sobbing uncontrollably and Jason and Terry were loving it. They slapped him and kicked his legs out from under him, all in front of a crowd of other kids. To Paul's dismay, he even spotted some of the Grade 9 girls in the crowd. As he lay there on the ground, Jason hoarked right in Paul's face. Terry just laughed.

Then Ian showed up. "What the fuck is this?"

Everybody turned.

By that time, Ian had a rep as a bad ass. He'd been suspended twice, once for shoving a teacher, the other time for being drunk at a school dance. He'd also been questioned by the principal and the police about a series of locker thefts, but nothing ever came of that. Still, there were about a dozen rumours going around about Ian, everything from him being a drug dealer to him knocking up one of the office secretaries to him being the illegitimate son of Paddy Mitchell, the notorious armed robber.

If they were aware of this, it didn't faze the two Grade 11 guys one bit.

"Fuck off you little shit or you'll get it too," Jason said, barely even glancing at Ian. Terry kicked Paul in the gut hard to emphasize his friend's point.

"All right then."

Ian didn't hesitate. He flew at the first guy, driving his fist into Jason's mouth. The guy was stunned and Ian took full advantage, grabbing him by the throat and landing three quick punches to his face. Jason fell to his knees, his hands clutching his nose and mouth, desperately trying to stop the bubbling blood.

Terry tried to grab Ian from behind, but it was too late, he was in a rage by then. He elbowed Terry in the stomach to back him off, then turned around and drove his foot into Terry's knee, bending it backwards. The sickening crack seemed to echo around the parking lot. Terry collapsed, his leg broken.

Ian was pumped, his eyes darting around the parking lot, looking for another fight. Jason wisely stayed down while Terry was holding his leg, moaning for help. Ian helped Paul up and they walked away.

"Holy *shit*," said Paul, laughing and crying at the same time, wiping snot and dirt from his face. "You killed them! You kicked their ass! I owe you, thank you, I'll do anything . . . "

"Yeah, yeah," groaned Ian. "We gotta get me to a fucking hospital. I think I broke my hand."

Terry and Jason were each suspended a week for the fight. With his reputation, Ian was gone for the rest of the year and was told to find another school in the fall. He didn't care one bit.

The next year, Ian found a technical school downtown that would let him in. Paul was pretty much at his beck and call—and loving it. He wrote essays for Ian, let him crash at his house a couple of times, and generally did whatever Ian asked of him.

In return, Ian invited him out to a couple of parties and even got Paul laid for the first time. There were five or six of them drinking at Ian's apartment. A girl thought Paul was cute in a homely kind of way, and Ian let her know that he was also a virgin. She found that irresistible and after another couple of drinks, Ian shoved them both into his bedroom and turned off the lights. Paul was terrified but the girl knew exactly what to do.

Paul walked a bit taller after that night and swore to himself again that he would never let Ian down. Of course, even in Grade 9, before the fight, Paul had known Ian was into some bad shit. He'd heard the rumours and even believed some of them. He knew Ian had a lot more money on him than a guy who didn't have a job should, and he'd seen Ian driving a bunch of different cars, guessing correctly they were stolen. After the fight, Ian didn't even try to hide it from Paul. He told him about the break-and-enters, he told him about ripping off delivery trucks, he told him that if he ever needed any pot or acid, Ian would hook him up.

Paul was sure it was something that would pass, that Ian would straighten himself out. He always thought Ian was smart enough to go a long way if he ever applied himself. Those hopes were shot down when Ian dropped out of high school at 16.

They saw each other a couple of times a year after that, in bars, at hockey games, or just downtown. Ian was always well dressed, surrounded by tough-looking guys, and had a lot of money to flash around. It made Paul feel good just to know somebody like that. Then Paul lost touch for a couple of years when he went away to university in 1991.

When he moved back to Ottawa in the spring of 1996 to work for a high-tech firm, he tried to look up Ian again, but couldn't find him. He checked around with some people from high school, and there were always "Ian sightings," but Paul could never manage to hook up with his old friend.

Even though Paul had known about Ian's bad side, it was still a shock to him when he picked up the paper one morning that summer and there, with a bold headline, was a story detailing how Ottawa-Carleton police had captured his old friend. And they were calling him a "one-man crime spree."

$ $ $

When Paul had left town to go study in 1991, Ian had taken on a different type of education. He'd met a bunch of guys from the west end who were pulling serious commercial break-and-enters. The guys would go in through the roofs of drug stores or shopping centres, drop down into the manager's office and pluck the safe out. They were netting serious, serious money—$35,000, $45,000, even $70,000 a job. They ran by the name the "Champagne Gang" because they used their money to live such a lavish lifestyle—travel, cars, clothes and plenty of women.

At that time, Ian was still ripping off delivery trucks and storerooms, focusing mainly on stereos and computers. Ian and a buddy would make the circuit of big electronics stores early in the morning when deliveries were being made. They'd stake the situation out, figure out how many employees were working and then wait for an opening. As soon as the truck or the warehouse was left unattended, they struck, grabbing a couple of boxes and throwing them in the back of Ian's Chevy Blazer.

Ian hated doing these jobs. He thought they were petty and he never made much money off them, but as his buddies always said, it beat working nine to five.

Ian fenced the computers and stereos to a couple of Lebanese guys in the west end. As it happened, these were the same guys that the Champagne Gang used to fence the stamps and lottery tickets they stole from their rooftop jobs. Ian would run into them a couple of times a month at the Lebanese guys' place and soon they were drinking together. Ian quickly realized theirs was the kind of work he wanted.

There was a cardinal rule though: You could never ask somebody else how they did their job. That, however, wasn't a problem with the Champagne Gang. Once you had them out in a bar, got a couple of shooters into them and started complimenting their work, they'd open right up. After six months, Ian had picked up enough pointers to try a job of his own.

The technique was simple in theory. Most major stores had expensive alarm systems on their doors and windows to keep thieves from breaking in. Then, as a second line of defence, on the floor of the store they had a series of motion detectors that let out beams of light. If anybody crossed one of those beams, it would set off the store's quick response alarm and bring the cops running.

The store's final defence was the safe they kept the money and valuables in. The trick that Ian picked up from the Champagne Gang was to bypass the first two lines of defence and go straight for the safe.

In the spring of 1994, Ian took his Blazer out every second day, trying to find an easy score. He wanted to pull the job outside of Ottawa to limit the suspicion. He wanted a store near a major highway, so there would be an easy escape route. And he wanted a store with no high-rise buildings around it; he didn't want somebody in an eighth-floor apartment looking out and seeing him at work.

Once he found a suitable store, he had to go inside, find out where the safe was, spot all the motion detectors, and get a feel for how much cash business they did. He considered a Canadian Tire, he considered a CompuCentre, but he finally opted for a big Loeb supermarket in Pembroke.

The store was about two hours north of Ottawa and Ian figured that was perfect. He drove up there every day for a week, checking the store during the day and the streets at night to see how many police cruisers were around. The Champagne Gang had always told him the best time to strike was Sunday night because all of the weekend's receipts were in the safe. So, Ian decided, Sunday night it was.

He didn't want to risk stealing a car, so he took his Blazer, but splashed mud all over the car, with special emphasis on the licence plates to make them indecipherable. He drove past the Loeb, making sure there were no strange cars or security guards in the lot. Then, just before 1 a.m., he parked his Blazer behind the building.

Using the water pipes, he shimmied up the side of the building until he was on the roof. He wore a dark wind-breaker, black jeans and a baseball cap. His high school backpack was slung over his shoulder with a crowbar, tin-snips, screwdrivers, and other assorted tools inside. He had a pick-axe strapped to the backpack.

Once on the roof, Ian measured off where he thought the manager's office was. It took him more than an hour to cut through the roof, first using the pick-axe, then the crowbar and tinsnips. When he finally poked his head through, he realized how lucky he had been. He was right in the corner of the office. A couple of feet to his left, and he would have been looking down at the floor of the store and all the motion detectors that went with it.

Ian checked to make sure there were no motion detectors in the office—there weren't—and then slipped down into the hole. He hung from one of the ceiling beams and let himself drop to the floor of the office. No alarm sounded, so Ian made his way to the safe in the corner.

Ian had broken into a couple of safes in his day. Usually, the cheap ones were pretty simple. Slip the crowbar in between the door and the frame, take a couple of whacks with the hammer, pry at it a bit. Repeat the process a couple of times and you'd be inside. Only this safe looked a bit tougher. It was bigger and had solid steel walls. Still, Ian figured he could do it. How hard could it be?

An hour later, Ian knew exactly how hard it could be. Try *impossible*.

It was after 3 a.m. and he'd made zero progress on the safe. Ian leaned against the wall, exhausted. He dreamt of water, Gatorade, juice, anything to drink. He had to make a decision. He couldn't lift the safe, no way, not by himself. And he couldn't get in. He had to bail.

The drive back to Ottawa was as depressing as it got for Ian. All that work for nothing. Three nights later, when he was out for drinks with a couple of friends at Stoney's, it got even worse. A bunch of guys from the Champagne Gang were there. Ian told them the whole story and they laughed for 15 minutes. Ian wanted to crawl away and hide.

Instead, a couple of the guys took pity on him. Sometimes, Ian discovered, the gang did side work. They always needed a reliable guy to keep six—watch out for cops and security—or help dig a hole through the roof. They said they'd take Ian along a couple of times, show him the ropes.

A couple of months later, Ian went out on a job with two of the guys from the gang. The target was a K-Mart in Trenton. It was the same routine. Up on the roof, cut through into the manager's office, get into the safe. Ian watched the guys work in awe. They were quick and tenacious as they attacked the safe. In less than 30 minutes, the door swung open. There was $18,000 cash inside. It was small fry compared to the Champagne Gang's usual scores. But for Ian it was pure bliss.

By the end of 1994, Ian was going out on his own. He'd pulled four jobs, this time with the help of his old partner from the delivery-truck jobs. He made more than $70,000 that year, tax free, and was living life as it was meant to be lived: eating out every night, jumping down to New York to see some shows with his girl, buying the $2,000 guitar he'd always had his eye on. He only needed to do a job every month, seeing as he was taking in at least $10,000 a score.

The next year, 1995, was a banner year. Ian pulled another 15 jobs, this time grabbing as much as $48,000 from a single safe. He'd gotten the routine down and was getting in and out faster than he ever had before. Ian estimated he took in more than $250,000 that year, though he didn't have much to show for it—he'd started to spend a lot of money on cocaine. Not that he liked the drug much, but Ian had quickly figured out that there was no faster route into a girl's pants than through a white line up her nose. Out every night, scouting out jobs on weekends, for Ian it was the life. The days of ripping off computers from delivery trucks were a distant and painful memory.

Then, in July 1996, he got caught.

It was stupid, really. Ian had gotten lazy. The gang had always told him to use a third person, a driver and six-man, so the car wasn't parked behind the store where it could arouse suspicion. Ian usually went without, not wanting to cut up the take one more time.

Sure enough, there he was, pulling a drug store job out in one of Ottawa's suburbs. When he and his partner popped out of the hole, there was a squad car in the lot below, running the plates of Ian's brand new Jeep Cherokee. The cop heard the movement on the roof, called for backup and Ian and his partner were pinched. The next day, investigators tried to connect another dozen or so jobs to Ian. The investigators boasted to the newspaper reporters that they had captured one of Ottawa's most prolific thieves. A one-man crime spree.

When Paul read about Ian's exploits in the newspaper, he drove up to visit him in jail. It was a bizarre reunion, Ian wisecracking like always, Paul easily falling into the old routines of the relationship.

As for the charges against him, Ian didn't play any games. He'd pleaded guilty to more than a dozen break-and-enters and been given an 18-month jail sentence. He admitted to Paul he'd done the crimes.

"Yeah, what's the big deal? I didn't hurt a soul, not a soul," he'd say, sloughing off any criticism.

Paul thought this out. It was true—Ian had only pulled jobs at stores, never at somebody's home. He never actually threatened anybody or held them hostage. Hell, because all the jobs were done at night, he never even saw anybody. So what was the big deal?

"What about the businesses you hit?" asked Paul after some more thought. "What about the people who owned them?"

"You sound like the cops. That's what they kept going on about. Come on, Paulie, really bud—these are big chains, they have lots of money. Besides, they all have insurance for these things."

Then, Ian checked around the jail's visiting room to make sure nobody else was listening. He leaned in and started talking in a low whisper.

"Look, you should see some of the guys in here. One guy, he fucking split open a lady's head when she was coming out of the bank machine. The lady was like 80 years old. It was in the newspaper and everything. Another guy, Johnny, he walked into a fucking Mac's Milk store with a machete. A fucking *machete!* For what? They never keep more than $100 in their cash anyway. Fuck. Come on, bud."

Paul could only smile. Leave it to Ian to rationalize his way out of this. But even Paul had to admit it: He was a lot happier to be visiting his old friend Ian the thief than his old friend Ian the rapist or murderer.

Paul ended up visiting Ian about twice a month, talking about old times, shooting the shit. Paul started running a couple of errands for Ian on the outside, and on several occasions, delivered some money that Ian owed to bookies. It made Paul feel good that for once, it was Ian who needed *his* help.

Ian ended up serving 12 months of his 18-month sentence. He could have been out a lot earlier, but as usual, Ian just couldn't keep himself in line.

In Canada, there are two types of sentences—penitentiary and provincial. If a criminal gets any sentence less than two years, they serve it in a provincial jail. The jails tend to have a better atmosphere, more facilities and focus on rehabilitating the inmates through school and counselling. If a criminal gets a sentence of two years or more, he's sent to a federal penitentiary. This is considered hard time and any rookie knows he's crossed the line when does his first pen bit.

When somebody gets nailed with a provincial sentence, like Ian, it's measured in thirds. An inmate can apply for parole after serving one-third of his sentence. As in all sentences, inmates are guaranteed to be released after serving two-thirds of their sentence. The only time an inmate is forced to serve the full term is if the parole board makes a "dangerous offender" application and wins the argument that the criminal is so dangerous they should be kept inside.

In Ian's case, with good behaviour, he could've been released six months into his sentence. But he got in a couple of "beefs," as the fights are called in the inside, and he mouthed off to a couple of guards. Then, when he was up for parole, Ian showed "a total lack of remorse for his crimes." At least, that's the way the parole board described it.

So Ian was forced to do the mandatory 12 months. And truth be told, he kind of enjoyed it. There was a good floor hockey league, a top-notch weight room, and a bunch of good guys in the joint with him.

When Ian finally got out in March 1998, Paul swore he would do anything to help him go straight.

$ $ $

Ian doesn't show up for the resumé session at Paul's on Sunday morning until 11:30. This is nothing unusual. Punctuality is not one of his strong suits.

"Sorry about that," Ian says as he ambles in and drops himself onto the couch. "Late night."

"That's okay. Anything happen? Meet anyone?"

"Bud, I swear, you should've seen it. I'm dancing with this girl, I'm just whipped, I can barely stand. I don't know what I'm doing but she starts kissing me! No word of a lie, bud, I couldn't believe it. Then I got this other yummy chick's number too. I could've gone home with her too, I swear, I was just too drunk. I don't know what it is with these girls, bud. They were all over me last night."

"You have the touch. You're the bad boy," laughs Paul. "Women love the bad boys."

"I guess so. I swear, it's sick. *Sick.* I gotta slow down."

Yeah right, thinks Paul. That's the last thing you're going to do.

It was a Sunday morning, and there were another two NFL playoff games on that day. Since Ian needed help with a resumé, they had agreed to work on the computer in the morning and then watch the games together in the afternoon. Ian had won on the Denver game yesterday and was letting the money ride on the Vikings game. Paul had made a couple of bets on Pro-Line himself.

Ian figured it was time to get a real job. Since he'd gotten out of jail 10 months earlier, he'd worked exactly three days, one of them filling in as a waiter at his buddy's restaurant and the other two days that week as an extra in the movie.

That was going to change though. Ian had made a New Year's resolution to find a job by the end of January.

"What better way to start 1999, eh bud?" says Ian. "It's like a fresh start. I can put all of last year behind me."

Paul's guardedly optimistic as they start that morning. Only the day before, Ian had been wistfully talking about pulling jobs for $150,000. Still, he seems genuine as they sit down at the computer together.

Surprisingly, Ian isn't that picky about his work. For the moment, he'll take anything, so long as it pays at least $12 or $15 an hour. Well, almost anything. He doesn't want to do manual labour outside or in a public place. But he will do factory work or get a job in a warehouse.

"People might drive by and spot me. I don't want anybody to see me, see what I've been reduced to," Ian says. "I mean, come on, some of the guys would give me a hard time. I don't think I could take that."

Deep inside, Ian harboured dreams of working in television or the movies. Not necessarily on screen right away, but maybe behind the scenes.

"A 'grip.' What the hell does a grip do?" wonders Ian. "I bet I could do that."

Paul liked to think he was a pretty creative guy, but even he is having problems with Ian's resumé. The guy is 25 and all he has is a Grade 9 education and no prior work experience. He hasn't even held a steady job since he pedaled around an ice cream bike when he was 11.

"We could fudge the dates for the ice cream job a bit, make it 1994 instead of 1984," muses Paul. "We could call it marketing and sales. It might work." Paul thinks some more. "And your friend at the bar. He'd say you managed the restaurant for a while, right? That would look good. And we could say you took a year at college. Nobody checks that stuff."

Ian squints at the computer screen. So far, his resumé consists of his name, address and phone number.

"Who are you kidding?" he finally says. "I mean, come on—how am I going to get one of these jobs? Who are we kidding?"

"Yeah, but you've got to start somewhere. What the fuck, so you rough it for a while, get something, anything . . ."

Ian looks down at his hands. "Maybe this isn't right for me. Maybe this whole scene isn't right for me."

"What are you talking about?"

"Look, I'm just saying, What if? What if I got pinched again? For a break-and-enter, what would I be looking at? A fin—tops. What would I serve?"

Paul is silent. There's no point in arguing.

"Vancouver would be nice," Ian says in a distant voice. "I could just get away. Start over. Maybe open a bar, if I had enough money."

Ian gets up and pulls on his leather jacket.

"Where you going?" asks Paul. "What about the game?"

"Forget about it. I'll catch it somewhere else."

"Yeah, okay."

And then Ian is gone.

$ $ $

One big chunk. That's all Ian figured he needed to make a clean break from crime. He kept on telling himself that if he could just pull one more job, that would be it—enough money to start a business, get an education, whatever. He'd started thinking about it a couple of months ago, but the resumé disaster that morning had brought it home hard: there was no other way.

The thing that had stopped him before was picking the job. What would give him a big enough chunk? He couldn't go back to doing a drug store or an IGA. What did they have? Fifty-thousand, tops. Banks and MoneyMarts had the cash inside, but they were out of the question. With their security and safes, you couldn't get into them at night. Ever. The other option was to just walk through the front door with a gun, but for what—a measly $2,000? That just wouldn't be enough.

The idea had come to Ian right after Christmas. Where would there be a lot of cash? The Price Club.

It was obvious. Ian's aunt shopped there all the time. It was cash only; no credit cards, no cheques. That meant the safe would be full. On a Sunday night after a busy weekend? Conservative estimate—$100,000; Ian's guess—$150,000.

He started out a couple of weeks before by visiting the store a few times during the day, then driving by it at night, just to check it out. It was a good security setup, but not invincible. He could do the job, with a little help from some friends. That weekend, when he was supposed to be thinking about the resumé and straight jobs, all he could think about was the Price Club.

After leaving Paul's place on Sunday morning Ian went over to his old partner's house. He laid out the plan and the partner was in.

Next Ian needed to find a "six-man," somebody to keep watch outside the Price Club while he and his partner did the dirty work. Ian had a buddy he'd met on the inside, a stand-up guy who could be trusted. A quick phone call and he was in too. They were ready to go.

It was frosty cold that Sunday night as they left Ian's place. The six-man dropped Ian and his partner a block away and then stationed himself across the street from the Price Club where he had a clear view of the store. The six-man had a cellphone and Ian kept one too. If trouble hits, if the cops start sniffing around, the six-man calls Ian inside and they rock out of there quick.

The next step was to breach the live security. The Price Club has a paid security guard who watches the outside of the store at night. He sits in an unmarked car parked out front, and every hour he makes a tour, driving around the Price Club's parking lot, looking for suspicious activity.

So Ian grabs his partner and the two of them wait around the corner of another building, about five hundred yards away from the Price Club. When the security guard stops his car out front by the main entrance after a round, they circle the store and come up behind. They shimmy up the pipes, wearing nothing but black, bags of tools strapped to their backs. They're each wearing gloves.

On top, Ian uses the cellphone to call the six-man, making sure everything's clear. Then he marks off the roof in paces, measuring twice, finding the exact spot on the roof that would be right above the Price Club's office complex at the back of the store. The two of them attack the roof, one with the pick-axe, the other with the crowbar. They knock through the gravel and tar, cut away at the metal and wood, until they have a hole to slip through.

The partner stays on the roof while Ian lowers himself to the metal girders that criss-cross the ceiling. Immediately below Ian is the top side of the store's ceiling panels.

Ian has to be careful. The ceiling is made up of squares of light tile not much sturdier than Styrofoam that are laid across a metal frame. One wrong step and he falls through, like a kid who wanders out on the pond's thin ice during spring thaw. If he fell, he'd hit the floor and break a leg, not to mention set off about a dozen motion detectors and sound guard alarms. On his knees now, Ian carefully pries up one of the gypsum squares. He lifts it aside gently, and lowers his head through.

In the office are three safes, each identical in size, on the wall opposite from the office's door. The bad news is that there are motion detectors coming from just above the office door, their beams forming a protective ring around the safes.

Ian closes his eyes and clenches his jaw. Think. Just like old times, says Ian. There's *always* an angle.

He has it.

Ian moves back a couple of feet and pulls himself half-way up and out of the hole.

"Is everything clear?" he asks his partner.

"Looks like it." His partner dials the cellphone. The six-man gives the clear sign too.

"Let's go, we got an angle."

They both go back down through the hole in the roof and gingerly step along the beams.

When Ian gets to the office, he creeps a couple of feet further, past the back office wall where the safes are lined up.

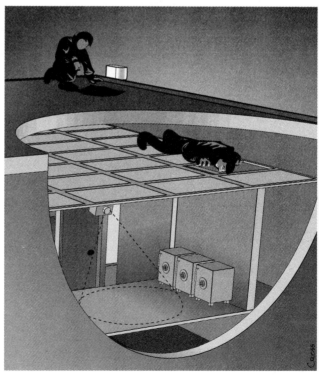

He gets down, pries up one of the ceiling panels, and pokes his head through. Below him is a hallway that separates the office and a changing room. There are a couple of motion detectors in the hallway, but only near the doors — nothing along the back wall of the office. Ian and his partner drop down to the hallway floor.

Silence for a half-minute. No clicks of alarms, no flashing lights on the motions, no distant sirens. The cellphone doesn't ring either. Ian knows they are clear.

They turn their attention to the back wall of the office. Cheap gyp rock covering a tin frame. No problem. It takes Ian and his partner just ten minutes with the pick-axe and the crowbar to tear apart the gyp rock and crumble away the wall. They bend the tin frame aside like putty. There are the backs of the three safes, perched in a row like sitting ducks.

The plan was to pull them back out of the office, but the safes are heavy as hell. The two men can't budge them. So Ian takes out a rope from his bag, ties it around safe number one. Then he and his partner lean back and push off with their legs, as if they're in a tug of war. The safe tips over and comes sliding out of the office. The beams from the motion detectors fall harmlessly inches away from the front of where the safe had stood.

Working together in silence, they start on the first safe. It's concrete covered in tin, a typical store safe. Some stores use all-steel safes, but if there's a fire, the safe heats up and the money can burn. A concrete safe, covered in metal, gives you heat protection, so your money's a bit safer. At least from natural disasters.

Ian slams his pick-axe into the small seam between the door of the safe and the body of the safe. The metal ripples a bit. A couple of more blows and the metal surface is really starting to give. Now Ian can fit the tip of the crowbar under the lining. He pries it back to uncover the concrete wall of the safe. Then Ian starts to hammer at the concrete, banging away until it starts to crumble. He delicately slides the broken pieces out bit by bit, kind of like taking apart a puzzle.

Thirty minutes of that and you've got a gaping hole on one side of the safe. Another ten minutes' work and you can pop the door.

Safe number one takes forty minutes and it's a bonanza: Thick plastic envelopes of money, each in different denominations. A computerized sticker shows the amount in each bundle. All the bundles have four-figure stickers. A couple—the hundreds and the fifties—have five-figure stickers on them.

Then the joke. This was just like the old days for Ian. The safe was actually a pretty good one. Inside the main concrete chamber, along the floor, was a smaller, steel safe, built into the walls of the main frame. It took up about a sixth of the space inside the safe and for guys like Ian, it was impossible to break into.

The thing was, the stores never used that inside safe. It's too small to keep all the money in, and the managers can't be bothered using two combinations every time they have to put something in-side. All the goodies are just stacked up on top of the inside safe. It's almost sad; the manufacturers go to all that trouble to build a better safe and the stores are too lazy to even use it properly.

Ian and his partner undo the rope and tie it around the second safe inside the office. In another forty minutes, that one's open too. Then the third.

Almost three hours have passed since they first started digging the hole in the roof. Ian takes all the cash and stuffs it into his backpack. They climb back up onto the beams and go out through the hole in the roof.

It's almost 4 a.m. Getting late.

Ian dials the six-man. The security guard was due for a round in fifteen minutes. Ian decides to wait until after the round. He doesn't want the guard to go early and catch them climbing down the building.

After the guard makes his hourly drive around the mall, Ian and his part-ner slither down the pipes. The tools are all left on the roof or in the office. They'd been wiped clean of prints when the evening started. The two men run across the street to where the six is parked.

"Fucking *yes*! Fuck. That was easy. *Fuck*." His partner's in the back seat shouting, adrenaline pumping, high on crime. The driver, the six-man, is still paranoid, eyes on the rearview mirror, constantly shoulder-checking as he drives away.

They arrive safely back at Ian's place. It's his job, so he does the counting.
One forty two.
$142,000.
142 large.
Ian smiles "till his face hurt."

$ $ $

Ian didn't call Paul at all that week. Paul shrugged it off. His old friend had never been the reliable type.

It's the end of January when he gets the postcard. It was from Vancouver, no return address, no name of the sender. The card has a picture of the mountains. When he reads the note on the back, Paul can only laugh—

Paulie:

Don'T Think I'll be needing The resume

A PAGER, A GOLD CARD, AND A STRAWBERRY IMAC: A DAY IN THE LIFE OF A CREDIT CARD CON MAN

Nick likes to think of himself as a man of many talents and charms, but deep down he knows his true gift is his uncanny ability to come up with credit card numbers.

It's like magic. He gets to know somebody at a party, or starts chatting them up at a mall, and next thing you know, they're friends—and Nick's new friends are always open to suggestions on how to make a little extra cash on the side. Over the past five years, he'd built up a whole network of contacts this way: waiters, store clerks, bank tellers, gas attendants—hundreds of people in low-paying jobs who weren't above making a dollar. Each person knew that if they managed to get a credit card number from an unsuspecting customer and called Nick quick, it'd be an easy $100, or even better, $200 if the number was from a gold card.

Each day Nick makes the circuit in downtown Toronto, cruising from store to store, mall to mall, visiting old contacts and trying to make new ones. The whole time, his pager buzzes relentlessly as contacts call in to report a score. They were smooth transactions: Nick meets them, jots down the cardholder's name, credit card number, and the card's expiry date in a little black book, then a couple of bills are slipped back the other way. VISA, MasterCard, American Express—they're all fine with Nick.

Nick is usually just the go-between, reselling the numbers to a group who print fake cards with them or use the numbers on the Internet. But if he needed something, Nick would occasionally dip into the stash himself.

Today, he needs a computer.

It's a Thursday morning and Nick strides into a Yonge Street computer store, turning a couple of heads as he does so. He's a handsome man, six feet four inches, strong features, smooth dark skin from his Jamaican roots. Nick knew the importance of appearance; the last thing he would do is draw heat by walking into a store dressed like a street thug. Today, he's wearing a soft brown leather jacket from Roots, a beige wool turtleneck from Hermes, khakis, and some lush Prada shoes. He looks good and knows it. Sometimes, because of the colour of his skin and the size of his body, people ask him if he plays for the Raptors or the Argos. Nick likes that.

As he enters the store, an overly earnest sales clerk is at his side immediately. The clerk is almost a foot shorter than Nick, a bit chubby, his shirt and tie straight from the discount bin at Tip-Top. There's a shine of sweat on the young man's forehead. It's a bit after 9 a.m., and the clerk's dark hair is still wet from his morning shower. At least Nick hoped it was from the shower. No man should sweat that much.

"What can I help you with today?" the clerk asks, adjusting his tie, trying to size up the customer.

"I need a computer," Nick answers. "I'm pretty much looking for a complete system. My business is expanding, I'm opening a second office, just around the corner actually, on King."

As he speaks, Nick runs his finger over the strawberry iMac on display at the front of the store, admiring its design. He'd seen them advertised on television, but never up close. They were smooth.

The clerk leads Nick past rows of software to the back of the store where all the PC computer systems are set up. As they walk, the clerk's forehead creases as if he is trying to calculate his potential commission off the sale.

"We have a lot of good deals, a lot of packages," the clerk says, his arm sweeping the room. "What do you need? Mostly word processing? Graphics? What's your business?"

"I guess you could say my business is providing talent. I work with studios, advertising agencies, whatever," Nick says, flashing his business card. "We need the usual system, word processing, spreadsheet, scanner, Internet hook-up.

The clerk takes the business card from Nick, notes the address, and slips it into his shirt pocket.

"So, you come from Montreal?"

"Just came down. Love that city. They have a scene there. A couple of movies being shot, lots of television work and commercials. My people are busy. But if you want to make it in entertainment . . ."

" . . . you have to come to Toronto," the clerk finishes. "No kidding. Business is good?"

"*Very* good," Nick says, letting the word "very" hang in the air like expensive perfume.

The manager of the store was arranging papers at the cash register. Having overheard the conversation, the man looks up and nods approvingly at the possibility of a big sale.

"Need any help Kevin?" the manager asks the clerk.

"We're okay."

Nick continues. "I already have an office in Montreal. It's very smooth. We have a Pentium III, printer, scanner, the whole thing. I want pretty much the same."

"What system do you have already? IBM? Mac?"

The clerk takes out a paper napkin from Harvey's and wipes the sweat off his forehead. Nick scans the room quickly, checking out the brand names.

"Compaq."

Kevin nods and begins running down the features of the package.

Fraud: The Legalities

CANADIAN CRIMINAL CODE, SECTION 380

(1) Every one who, by deceit, falsehood or other fraudulent means, whether or not it is a false pretence within the means of this Act, defrauds the public or any person, whether ascertained or not, of any property, money or valuable security.

  (a) is guilty of an indictable offence and liable to a term of imprisonment not exceeding ten years... (where the) value of the subject-matter of the offence exceeds five thousand dollars or

  (b) is guilty

    (i) of an indictable offence and liable to imprisonment for a term not exceeding two years, or

    (ii) of an offence punishable on summary conviction where the value of the subject-matter of the offence does not exceed five thousand dollars.

Pentium III, scanner, laser printer, 15-inch monitor, and a software bundle, all for $4,599, plus taxes.

Nick examines the computer before him. "I hate those tiny screens. Can we upgrade to something bigger?"

It was a set deal, so Kevin looks over at the manager who is still listening in. The manager pipes in, "Well, it's a package, but for you, we can add in a 17-inch monitor for only $300 more."

Nick smiles and nods. "No problem."

The manager and Kevin meet eyes. They love customers who don't haggle over price.

Nick pulls out his cellphone and dials a number. "James, Nick here . . . I've got a system just like the one in Montreal . . . Yeah, the price is fine. We can afford it, don't worry . . . No, no, I'll use the credit card . . . Just a sec." Nick covers the cellphone with his hand, and turns to the manager. "Can we take it with us right now?"

Kevin and the store manager bob their heads vigorously.

"Yeah, James, it's cool," Nick says. "You know the store, right near the

---

The Internet: Fraudster's Dream Come True

With the explosion of Internet-based businesses like amazon.com, more and more people are making credit card purchases online—and more and more fraud artists are scouring the 'Net for potential targets.

While most Internet business sites offer security protection and fraud coverage of up to $100 if a person's credit card number is lifted, that has done nothing to quell the fear of the average spender. According to an Angus Reid poll published in July 1999, more than half of consumers—52 per cent—are still leery of Internet transactions. Another 13 per cent said they were concerned about the privacy of personal information given out over the Internet.

The terrifying thing is that these people have reason to fear; on-line credit card fraud is on the rise and the security can be breached.

Need an example? For several days in July 1999, the customer database of MegaDepot, an online office supply dealer, was accessible through their web site. That meant the credit card numbers, expiry dates, addresses and phone numbers of more than 20,000 Canadians were available to anybody with a bit of computer know-how.

doughnut place . . . Yeah, that's the one . . . All right." Nick turns to the two other men. "My partner. He's setting up the office. He'll be right over with our van."

"Great, great, let's get this rung up," Kevin says as they make their way to the cash. "You know about the warranties, right?"

"I assume it's the standard . . ." Nick stops speaking as he approaches the cash register. He knows he shouldn't press, not with the sweaty clerk so on edge, but . . .

"Is something wrong?" Kevin asks.

The manager looks over, concern in his eyes.

"It's just that my sister, she's starting junior high this year," Nick says, turning around. His eyes rest on the strawberry iMac computer at the front of the room.

"She's moving here to Toronto with me. I think it's going to be hard for her, she doesn't really know anybody yet. I don't know if I can afford it, but I'm thinking maybe I should buy her something too. For school. Like that iMac."

The manager comes over, sensing another sale. "Absolutely, that's a great computer for kids. Very educational. It can be a kid's best friend."

Kevin nods enthusiastically. The manager bursts out with the rest of the sales pitch. "It's a great time to buy too. It's only $1,499. They're coming out with new models soon, so they've dropped the price."

"Fifteen hundred. Does that comes with everything?"

"Everything but a printer," Kevin answers.

"Okay, throw in a bubble-jet too. She's got to print her essays, right?"

The manager smiles at Nick again. "We have a special on software for students. It's a good package. It has an encyclopedia CD-ROM, it has a dictionary, a thesaurus, atlas . . . "

Nick smiles too. What the hell. "Throw that in too."

The manager comes over and puts his hand on Nick's shoulder. "It's a good buy."

Behind the cash, Kevin brings out his napkin again and wipes more sweat from his forehead.

"Business must be good mister—" Kevin pauses to look down at the name on the American Express Gold Card. "—Mr. Watson."

"As I said, it's *very* good."

The total comes to more than $7,400.

Kevin begins processing the transaction. The sweaty clerk knows exactly what to do.

$ $ $

"Smooth. So very, very smooth."

Nick is sitting in the passenger seat of his friend James' white van. The computers are in the back.

"It really went that good?" asks James.

"Except for that clerk. That Kevin kid. Man, I thought he was going to drown in his own sweat, you know what I mean? He was so nervous."

"Yeah, but he's going to get paid."

"Oh, he's going to get so paid," chuckles Nick.

In fact, they were driving over to Kevin's apartment right now to drop off the iMac.

Nick laughs again. Kevin had been as nervous as hell, but the clerk still shot him a dirty look when he'd ordered the strawberry iMac. The night before, Kevin specifically said he didn't care what colour he got, just as long as it wasn't the pink one. Served him right for not playing it cool.

James is fighting the morning traffic on Bay Street, looking to take a left on Bloor. Kevin lives in the Annex with a roommate and he had given Nick his keys with instructions to leave the computer in his bedroom.

Never again with Kevin, Nick promised himself. It had gone smoothly, of course, but that was all thanks to Nick. Kevin was sweating from the get-go. Good thing the dollar signs had clouded the manager's eyes or there could have been trouble.

Nick was a pro at this play by now. He'd used it dozens of times before; it was a much better alternative to the fake cards. Sometimes the fakes were unreliable, sometimes the clerk could spot the flaws in the card, and if you got caught with one of those babies, the police automatically know you're connected. So when Nick wanted to buy something, he had his own special system.

It was a neat trick. Nick took his own gold American Express Card and on the back, stuck a white sticker over the magnetic strip. On that white sticker, he wrote down one of the stolen credit card numbers he'd picked up, the card's expiry date, and the name of the legitimate card holder. Since he already had a network of hundreds of contacts who sold him stolen credit card numbers, all he had to do was make a prearranged visit to one of those contacts to make the purchase. It was like his own shopping network. If he needed a stereo, it was with Will over at Adventure Electronics; if it was clothes, it was Andrée over at Holt Renfrew. And if it was a computer, well, today it was Kevin.

The play was easy. You act like strangers, go through the sales song-and-dance, make sure you get the manager or another employee involved in the transaction so you don't raise too much suspicion if the cops ever come by afterwards. And then, boom, you make the move.

In the store, Nick had handed Kevin his card and Kevin had run it through the magnetic-code reader by the cash. Of course, the card didn't read—Nick had covered up the magna strip with the white sticker. So Kevin punched in the number manually—the stolen credit card number that was written on the sticker on the back. All forms were signed under the real card-holder's name—in this case, some guy named Watson—and the transaction was done. If police ever did come around, it'd be at least three weeks later, usually six. And by then, nobody could give a good description of Nick, least of all his accomplice, who would describe someone who looked like a cross between Little Richard and Mr. T to help throw off police.

Instead of the usual payment of $100 or $200 for the credit card numbers, Nick's contact got his or her choice of merchandise from the store. Kevin wanted an iMac. Preferably green or blue—lime or blueberry in iMac-speak. Definitely not strawberry. Nick killed himself sometimes.

It's just past 11 in the morning now and, as usual, traffic is tight on Bloor. James lights a cigarette as he listens to sports talk on the Fan. The Raptors are playing .500 ball, having beaten the Wizards the night before, and are now just one game back of a playoff spot. The Leafs are in the playoffs and play-ing their first game that night. On the radio, the sports announcer's going out

Give Them Credit

The total number of VISA and MasterCard cards in Canada topped 35 million in 1998—more than one for every citizen. When you add in the piles of credit cards that aren't issued by major banks—Bay cards, PetroCanada cards, Canadian Tire cards and of course, American Express, that number soars to more than 100 million cards.

But the majority of credit card transactions are conducted with Visa and MasterCard, and as the chart below shows, there's no sign that that's going to end any time soon.

VISA & MasterCard	October 1997	October 1998
Number of cards in circulation	31.9 million	35.3 million
Outstanding balances	$20.5 billion	$23.9 billion
Average sale	$82.50	$90
Fraud losses	$88 million	$104.8 million

(Source: The Canadian Bankers Association web site, July 1999, http://www.cba.ca/eng/Statistics/FastFacts/visamc.htm)

of his head with hyperbole, calling these the "glory days." As he drives, James nods in agreement with what the announcer says, chipping in once in a while with his own insights. "Carter's the man. Rookie of the year, baby, no doubt about it," or "That's right, CuJo's the answer. He'll take us there."

Nick just looks out the window, staring down the young women. It's almost end of April and the warm weather is finally starting to hit Toronto. That meant shorter skirts, lighter tops and more women on the streets. Nick catches sight of a blonde woman bending down to pick up a copy of the *Star*. Her navy skirt rides up her thighs, exposing delicate skin that hasn't been touched by the sun for months. Nick exhales slowly through pursed lips and slips off his Roots jacket, folding it carefully on top of the iMac box. He's a happy man.

For Nick, Toronto had become home. He'd lived here for almost 10 years now and liked to think he knew the city inside out. As a kid, he'd been all over—Montreal, Ottawa, Kingston, London, Windsor. Just his mom and him. She worked in hotels, cleaning rooms, and always seemed to think things would be a little bit better someplace else. The pay in Montreal was lousy, the weather in Ottawa was too cold, not enough black people in Kingston or London, and Windsor just wasn't her scene. It was shitty for Nick. Just as soon as he made friends, they were gone, back on the road.

Finally, when Nick was 19, the two settled in Toronto. His mom got a job at the Radisson downtown. Nick finished high school and then enrolled at George Brown College. They both loved it. A cosmopolitan city, more money for Mom, more action for Nick. The only problem for Nick was that more action meant he needed more money—much more money than he had.

The trouble started his first year at George Brown. He was 20 then and he'd gotten a decent student loan—$9,000—but that was gone in a couple of weeks. Nick had wanted to make an impression, so he bought new clothes and a car to get to and from school. Once tuition was paid, there just wasn't that much money left.

By October, he was looking for angles. His mom had gotten him a part-time job bussing tables in the restaurant at the Radisson, but it was proving to be a completely inadequate source of funds, and Nick detested the work.

It was Steve, a buddy he'd met at George Brown, who first told Nick about the card deal. They'd been hanging and Nick was complaining about his money situation, as usual. Steve said he might have an angle for him. There was this Chinese kid he went to high school with. For $500, he'd sell you a credit card with a minimum $2,000 limit on it. Steve had just bought one and had hooked himself up with a new CD player for his car, speakers, and a ton of music.

"It was $1,400 worth of gear, man. You can't go wrong."

A couple of weeks later, the day after payday, Steve and Nick were out when they ran into the card seller at a bar. His name was Vince, and he was a short Asian kid decked out in a black leather coat, black T-shirt, and black pants. The guy was twitchy, always looking around, and he had a cellphone glued to his hand. After some small talk, Nick asked to be hooked up with a

The amount lost to credit card fraud in Canada almost doubled in the late 1990s. In 1996, it was estimated there was $86 million in credit card fraud; in 1997, that number hit $127 million; and in 1998, it soared to $147 million.

But perhaps this climb in fraud isn't simply a result of greed. A 1996 study by the Canadian Centre for Justice Statistics notes that "generally, when the unemployment rate increases or decreases, the credit card fraud rate follows a similar pattern."

(Statistics Canada, Catalogue no. 85-002-XPE, Vol. 18, No. 4, p. 6)

Though we may expect credit card and other types of fraud to be a big city problem, statistics yield some surprises:

City	Population	Credit Card Fraud Rate*	Total Fraud Rate*
Toronto	4,410,269	77	238
Montreal	3,365,160	89	285
Vancouver	1,883,679	80	308
Edmonton	890,771	134	405
Saint John	129,380	190	410
St. John's	175,249	84	511
Victoria	315,168	133	521
Halifax	344,135	289	529
Thunder Bay	130,006	277	562
Saskatoon	223,524	327	591

*Rates are calculated based on 100,000 population
(Source: Canadian Centre for Justice Statistics, Uniform Crime Reporting Survey, 1996, quoted in Statistics Canada, Catalogue no. 85-002-XPE, Vol. 18, No. 4, p. 6)

card. Vince nodded, took Nick's phone number and said they'd meet later. He ended up buying a fake MasterCard from Vince for $400. He used the phony credit card once or twice, just enough to recoup what he'd paid. He hated it, that feeling, that anticipation at the cash when you were waiting for the card to be authorized. What if it got rejected? He'd look like a fool.

Even worse, what if there was a flag on the card number and the store clerk calls security or police? He'd get embarrassed and arrested. For Nick, the risk just wasn't worth it, so he never bought another card from Vince again.

He was still looking for angles though, anything to get out of cleaning dirty dishes off tables at his mom's hotel. A couple of months later, near Christmas, he was having a Friday night drink at the Bamboo and ran into Vince again. They started talking and maybe it was the two rye-and-gingers Nick had already had, but for whatever reason, he started telling Vince how much he hated using the fake card. Vince broke out laughing.

"Me, I never touch," Vince said in agreement, slapping Nick on the back. "Only for fools. Too much work, always worried. Not worth it."

It must have been the rye, because Nick pressed on.

"Well, what about you Vince, my smooth friend. How do you make your money?"

Vince looked around the bar. It was just before 1 a.m. and it was packed, a lot of women swaying to the sound of the reggae band on stage. He was drinking vodka-soda, and maybe he'd had one too many, or maybe he saw some potential in Nick right from the beginning, but for whatever reason, Vince answered the question.

"Sales and collections."

Vince went on to explain his gig. He was a middle man. He brought stolen credit card numbers to his uncle. His uncle gave him a stack of fake cards to sell to friends or others who could be trusted not to talk, or at least, not be able to track Vince down again if things went sour. For his work, Vince got a cut of every transaction.

"It's good money. It pays my Accord," said Vince.

"How much money is good money?"

Vince hesitated and scanned the bar again. His fingers were unconsciously tapping the key pad of his cellphone. "Fifteen hundred. Depends."

Nick tried to play it cool, tried to keep his excitement from showing. "Bro-*ther*," he whistled. "Are you guys hiring? That's serious coin."

Vince put down his vodka-soda and reached into his pocket. He produced a wad of cash and card with a phone number on it. "Page me."

Vince passed Nick the card and went to drop a couple of twenties on the table to pay for the drinks. Nick took the card, but stopped Vince's hand. "The drinks are on me, my friend. I'll call you tomorrow."

Vince smiled, lit a cigarette, and disappeared into the throng of bodies.

Of course, Nick didn't actually have the money to pay for the bill, but he'd met this girl Tara earlier in the evening and now he saw her again. She was wearing a short skirt and a crisp white blouse with enough buttons undone to hint at a magnificent pair of breasts. Nick waved her over and they ended up talking the rest of the night, even sharing a dance. By last call, Nick had managed to persuade the girl to pay the bill *and* accompany him home.

Nick ended up calling Vince the next day. They met and shot a game of pool together, Nick getting the rundown as Vince sunk ball after ball.

If Nick got a credit card number, the name of the card holder, and the card's expiry date, he was to page Vince, pronto. They had to be good cards, cards with profit potential. No point in grabbing the number of some university kid's card, what with its $500 limit that was likely already maxed out. The point was to get the card numbers of the middle-class people, the ones who paid their bills and had a couple of thousand dollars of credit to play with. The best was to get a gold card number. They were always a success.

Nick was supposed to get the card numbers any way he could—digging out old receipts from the garbage bins of stores or rental car places, going through the mail and grabbing people's bills, whatever. Vince would pay Nick $100 for a regular card number, $200 for a gold card. The secret was to strike quickly. He was to deliver the numbers as soon as he got them, so they could be turned into cards immediately.

Nick worked under Vince for almost a year-and-a-half. He soon realized he wanted no part of digging through trash or prying open other people's mail boxes. It seemed downright petty. But Nick had another angle. A better angle.

He'd always had a way with people. His mother always boasted he could charm a crab out of its shell. In school, he had girls writing his essays for him, guys fronting him money for lunch, teachers cutting him slack. Now he went to work setting up a system that capitalized on his charm. Nick started with the girls he dated. They were sweet, they usually worked in bars or at the mall, and they'd do just about anything for him. They were the ones who started feeding Nick credit card numbers they'd picked up from oblivious customers.

After that, Nick passed the word on to a couple of friends. If they could get a number, Nick would pay them fifty bucks. A hundred for a gold card. The word was out: Nick would pay cash for numbers. It took off from there.

By the end of his first year with Vince, Nick was scoring at least nine or ten good numbers a week. After payouts to the contacts, he brought home $600 cash a week, easy. It was smooth and Vince was extremely happy about his decision to bring Nick under his wing.

"You got to meet my uncle," Vince said over drinks one night, his arm over Nick's shoulder. "He wants to meet you. He loves you. You make him so much money. He always tell me, 'Find more like Nick. Find more like Nick.'"

Nick was flattered and the next week, he met the uncle at a restaurant on Spadina. That's when he found out how much money Vince was making off him.

The uncle was wearing a white sleeveless undershirt and stained grey pants. He walked hunched over and smiled a lot, exposing teeth more gold than white. Nick couldn't believe it. This was the guy Vince worked for? This was the guy who had his hand in thousands of fake credit cards?

The uncle started to talk.

Vince was going out to Vancouver for a while, to work with a cousin of the family in a new business. Nick was told not to ask about that. The uncle wanted Nick to keep working, but to report directly to him. Same routine, just drop the numbers at the restaurant.

"I'll pay you what I pay Vince," the uncle said.

Vince was getting $200 a card number and $300 for a gold. Nick shook his head. Vince had been making a fortune off Nick, $100 for every number he'd come up with. Still, Nick could only smile. The bottom line was, he was going to be making a lot more money now. And that was a very good bottom line.

$ $ $

James takes a right near the University of Toronto campus and drives until they spot Kevin's house.

It made Nick feel a bit sheepish whenever he was around U of T or York, or Ryerson, or any other school for that matter. After meeting Vince, he'd never gone back to college. Every year, his mom asked him when he was going to get an education and make her proud. Nick had enrolled in courses more than once, but never finished them. Never went to more than two classes, to be honest. And now, he was turning 30 soon. His mom was right. He needed an education. There just always seemed be something in the way.

"Gotta get me an education," he says to nobody in particular as James pulls up to the curb.

Nick promises himself—yet again—that he will look into the computer course. You pay $15,000, sure, but after one year, you're guaranteed a job. That would make his mom happy, a real job. He could even stop lying to her about this phony talent agency. Nick makes a mental note to call the school first thing the next morning, just as soon as he finishes setting up his new computer.

Kevin lived on the second floor of a three-storey, red-brick house that had been converted into apartments. Nick lets James carry the iMac while he works the keys. Nick knocks on the door of Apartment 2, but there's nobody home. He turns the key and swings open the door. It's typical student housing. Second-hand couch, battered television, a stack of newspapers on the floor and dishes in the sink. Kevin had told him to put the computer in the room with the life-size poster of Data on the door. Kevin then patiently explained to Nick that Data was a crew member of the new Star Trek. Look for a tall guy in a yellow shirt and weird skin, Kevin had said.

Nick shakes his head when he sees the poster. That must go over well with the women. He opens the door and James puts the computer, the printer and the software on the bed. There are Star Wars figurines on the desk and a stack of fantasy novels on the floor. Nick realizes that women likely didn't visit Kevin too often.

"Do you guys know Kevin and Greg?"

Nick turns around. It's a blonde girl, dressed in slippers, cut-off jean shorts and an oversized U of T sweatshirt. Even without makeup, she's stunning. She has a laundry basket in her arms and Nick couldn't help but notice a lacy black bra peeking out from underneath a bath towel.

James starts to sputter something, but Nick takes control.

"We're with Kevin. We work together. He just gave me the keys to drop something off." Nick holds up the keys and gives them a jingle as a sign of reassurance. "Hey, how come Kevin never told us there was such a beautiful woman in his building? I would have visited more often."

The girl scoffs, but in a gentle, friendly way. "Aren't you a piece of work," the girl says. "I just moved in upstairs last month. I barely know anybody here. My name's Julie."

"Nick. I'm Nick and this is my associate James. Maybe we'll see you around the building sometime?"

"Sure. Ask Kevin. We're having some people over Saturday night. Why don't you drop by?"

Nick flashes his most charming smile. "If you're going to be there, I wouldn't miss it for the world."

Julie blushes and leaves to do her laundry. Nick and James lock the apartment, grab a couple of grilled chicken subs and Brisk ice teas from Subway and then drive to Nick's place to drop off the Compaq.

$ $ $

Nick knew that he wasn't the most romantic of criminals. Truth be told, it hurt him. In the movies, it was always the hip young actors who played the roles of the dashing armed robbers or the sinister mob types. If—and this was always a big if—the movies even portrayed somebody in the credit card game, they were usually fat, middle aged and had no style. And they were never black.

Even though it lacked glamour in his mind, Nick liked the gig. The work was fine, just talking and messing around with people. And the money was good too. Last year there'd been an article in the *Star* about credit card fraud, an article Nick had clipped. It said that banks lost $80-million a year to credit card fraud, compared to just $4-million a year to hold-ups. He was on the money side of the game, no question.

Of course, he knew he would never get rich off it, not in his position. He'd never made more than $2,000 a week, and he mostly pulled in about half that. Still, Nick didn't mind. It meant the risks weren't as high either.

He'd only been arrested by police once, in 1997. He'd rung up a bunch of clothes at Club Monaco, with the help of his young friend Cindy who was a salesclerk there. The woman managing the store had been eyeing him suspiciously the whole time, but the transaction went through and he thought he was clean. Four weeks later, when the owner of the credit card got the bill, the manager got a call from VISA, asking about the transaction. She pressured Cindy and the dumb girl admitted to knowing Nick. Thankfully, Cindy hadn't given up the scheme, but the police did call Nick in for questioning.

Nick was facing a "fraud under $5,000" charge. Thankfully, Nick thought, he'd only bought $800 worth of clothes. If he'd been pinched with a bigger purchase, he could've been hit with fraud over. The detective laid out the evidence. They had the VISA receipt with a fake signature they could match to Nick's handwriting, the cop explained. And they had the girl.

"The clerk. Cindy Reid. She made a statement. She said you were the one who used the credit card."

"Yeah, so?"

"So, we've got you," the cop said. Then he launched into the typical routine: innocent victim, hard-earned money lost, violation of privacy, the whole nine yards.

"Man, don't give me that. VISA covers all that shit," Nick said, brushing off the cop's guilt trip.

The cop only smiled. "You don't want a criminal record, Nick. If you help us, we can help you. A record's going to stay with you your whole life."

Nick only shrugged.

"Don't think we don't know who you are. Don't think we don't know what you do," the detective told Nick. Then he launched into the conspiracy theory. The cop said Nick was connected to the Dai Heun Jai, the big-time Asian gang. The cops told Nick that the Dai Heun Jai, also known as the Big Circle Boys, were responsible for tens of millions in credit card fraud each year. The cops told Nick he'd better talk, better give up the people he was working for.

It was Nick's turn to smile. *As if.* As if he'd rat anybody out. As if they had any leverage on him. As if this was going anywhere. A tiny fraud charge like this? Nick knew he had nothing to worry about. He played it cool.

"I don't know what you're talking about," he said, his charm turned up high. "Big Circle *what*? As I told you . . ."

Nick's story was that his boy Ty had lent him a credit card to buy some new clothes. Ty told Nick it was his girl's dad's card and he had the okay to use it. You see, Nick explained, he'd just started a new job as a waiter. He had to look good, but the money wasn't coming in yet. How was he supposed to know it was a stolen card? Ty just told him to sign the name on the card and write the girl's dad a cheque when he had the money.

The cops wanted Ty's name and whereabouts. Nick couldn't quite recall those details. He got slapped with the fraud under $5,000 charge. A couple of thousand in lawyer fees later, the charge was stayed. He didn't even have to spend a day in jail.

That episode had scared Nick, but just a bit. He didn't know exactly who Vince's uncle was, didn't even know his real name. All Nick knew was that he had a stack of cash and always paid on time. It wouldn't surprise Nick if the uncle was with an Asian gang, but what did it matter? Nick didn't know and what he didn't know couldn't hurt him.

Besides, Nick figured even if he ever did go down for something really big, it wouldn't be that bad. There was another numbers guy in Toronto who had been taken down by police a couple of years ago, a guy named Boateng. He ended up getting charged with $270,000 worth of credit card fraud. The guy was Nick's age, had gone to Ryerson, caught on to the scam and then just lived the life using the fake cards. When the dust settled, Boateng was hit with more than 30 charges, including fraud and assault. All he ended up getting for the credit card scams was nine months. Nine months in jail.

Nick figured if he was ever pinched hard, he wouldn't get any more than that. And Nick knew he could serve nine months. Like *that*.

$ $ $

When they get back to Nick's place, they put the Compaq computer boxes on the living room table and eat the subs on the condo's balcony with the iced tea to wash it down. In the distance, boats skip across the surface of Lake Ontario.

Nick checks his messages—his mom has called twice since breakfast—and then turns his pager back on. He'd forgotten he'd turned it off at the computer store. Eleven pages have built up, eight of them from contacts. Over the years, Nick has learned that only about 50 per cent of the calls from contacts ended up with him writing another number in his black book. Still, it wasn't a bad day. A new computer and probably four new numbers to sell to Vince's uncle.

After the subs and iced tea are done, James gets up to go. "Do you need me for anything else, bro?"

"We're clear," Nick says, pulling out a money clip and handing James two fifties. "That's all right. Thanks for your help."

"Anytime, man. As soon as you get some games set up, I'm coming over. I want to check out that John Madden football."

Nick promises to call James later and closes the door after him. He should've asked James to wait around and drive him back to the computer store so he could return Kevin's key. But the day is still warm and it's only a 35-minute walk. The fresh air will do him good.

On the way over, he stops at the Eaton Centre to meet one of his contacts. A girl in the men's department smiles at him and tells Nick that at lunch she sold a patent lawyer two Hilfiger shirts. He had a gold card.

Nick breaks into a wide grin. "Nathalie, Nathalie, Nathalie. You are looking good, as always."

Nathalie lifts herself up on her toes and returns Nick a wide smile. "Did you get it?"

"I paged you didn't I?" Nathalie answers sassily.

Nick leans in and kisses her on the lips. "Baby, you're the best."

Nathalie takes a smoke break and they walk out into the mall. Nick jots the number down and passes the girl a hundred and two fifties.

"Thanks, baby. We've got to get together sometime, we'll get something to eat, hang out a bit . . . "

Nick lets the words fade and turns to leave. But the girl puts her hand on his shoulder. She's a young Jewish girl, totally straight. Nick met her at the Second Cup the month before. She loves the game, loves the idea of doing something bad.

"Nick, that sounds really good. Call me. Really."

Nick sizes her up. Why not? "What are you doing after work?"

"Nothing that important."

"I'll pick you up after your shift." Nick kisses her again and leaves. Why not, indeed.

It's a short walk back to the computer store. The manager waves happily when he sees Nick.

"Back already?"

"Can't get enough."

Nick walks to the back where Kevin is working. They shake hands, Nick squeezing Kevin's apartment key into his palm. Kevin discreetly pockets it.

"You got me the pink one," Kevin whispers. "You bastard!"

Nick cracks another broad smile. "I met Julie at your place. Very nice."

"Oh, man," Kevin whines. "Please don't, she's so nice. I think I have a shot—"

Then the manager wanders back and it's time to get back to the script.

"Look, I can't find my receipt," Nick says.

Kevin shakes his head and goes back to playing the game. "Don't worry, I can give you another copy."

They go to the cash and Kevin fishes out the original copy of the sale. He passes it to Nick and Nick risks a wink.

As he leaves the store he nods to the manager again.

"Anytime you need anything . . ."

" . . . I'll come here," says Nick.

He leaves the store and heads back down Yonge Street. It's almost five now and the streets are coming alive. The Leafs play the Flyers in less than two hours at the Air Canada Centre and the bars are filling up with after-work drinkers. There's a definite buzz in the air.

Nick inhales deeply. He loves this city.

He strides off, wondering where he would take Nathalie that night.

MONEY FOR NOTHING: MAKING AND LOSING A MILLION, ONE CIGARETTE AT A TIME

It's a warm May morning. Wispy white clouds stretch overhead, and the sun's rays break into a thousand shards of light as they hit the St. Lawrence River. It feels as if there is no more peaceful place on Earth than the quiet eastern tip of Cornwall Island.

This beautiful, raw piece of land is something of a geographical marvel. The dark waters that roll eastwards past Cornwall Island are the spot where international borders converge. With a strong arm, a person standing on the eastern end of the island can lob stones into Quebec, Ontario and New York State; all three territories converge just off the island's rocky shores.

On the Canadian side of the river, near the city of Cornwall, children are kicking a soccer ball in Lamroureux Park, a long swath of public land that hugs the St. Lawrence. On the U.S. side, in the quiet village of St. Regis, worshipers slowly enter a graceful stone church that rises just yards from the water's edge.

The river appears to wander harmlessly past the small, emerald islands clustered here, yet another checkpoint for the St. Lawrence as it makes its way from the Great Lakes, past Kingston and Montreal, finally gliding by Quebec City and greeting the Atlantic Ocean.

As the sign in one highway-side store reads, "Welcome to our patch of paradise."

But like the calm surface of the St. Lawrence, looks can be deceiving. Just as the river's deep waters are home to ferocious currents and deadly undertows, this patch of paradise has its troubles too. This tranquil spot is actually a modern-day version of the Wild West, a smugglers' paradise where more than a billion dollars' worth of black-market goods move back and forth across the border each year. From cigarettes and alcohol, to cocaine and guns, to contraband freon gas and illegal aliens, the river has seen it all.

Part of the problem is the spaghetti of borders that divide this area. You have the Canadian provinces of Ontario and Quebec, the state of New York, and the countries of Canada and the United States. To further complicate matters, this is the home of the Akwesasne Territory, land governed and policed by the Mohawks. The reserve sits on the very hub where Canada and the U.S. meet, taking in some of Quebec, some of Ontario and some of New York State. It means there are more than a dozen different law enforcement agencies at work here: the Ontario Provincial Police, the Cornwall city police, the Royal Canadian Mounted Police, the Sûreté du Quebec, the Mohawk police, the New York State police, the Canadian customs officers, the American customs officers, and then the myriad of federal American agencies like the FBI and the DEA. Each group has to work within certain political boundaries and must stop at certain lines. Smugglers heed no such rules and it often makes for a one-sided battle.

Another part of the problem is the ever-changing system of tariffs and embargoes the governments of the various countries, provinces and the state choose to adopt. Cigarettes and alcohol are much cheaper in the United States than in Canada, so a fortune can be made by smuggling these goods north of the border and selling them on the black market. Likewise, items like Persian carpets made in Iran and cigars made in Cuba can be bought in Canada but not in the United States, so they form a steady stream of traffic the other way. If one set of rules and tariffs were in place for both countries, the majority of the smuggling would be stopped; there would simply no longer be a profit in it.

The biggest part of the problem, though, is human nature. People are drawn to money like mosquitoes to warm blood, and this is a spot rich in ways to make money. The RCMP have identified agents of Asian gangs, New York Mafioso, and Colombian drug cartels all working in this little area, all drawn to the money.

How lucrative is the smuggling here? Ask Larry Miller.

Miller was a small-time bar owner in Massena, New York, just across the river from Cornwall, who happened to have a keen businessman's instinct. In the late '80s he began to see the profits that could be made by transporting cheap cigarettes and alcohol across the border into Canada. He was only one of hundreds of smugglers when he began, but he ended up building the biggest empire of them all. American authorities say his organization alone smuggled $687 million U.S.—more than $1 billion Canadian—worth of contraband cigarettes and alcohol into Canada through the Mohawk reserve between 1991 and 1997. The profits were staggering. Miller owned mansions in Las Vegas and New York, was a partner in a Moscow casino with Hollywood action star Chuck Norris, and flew around the country in his personal Lear jet.

When he pleaded guilty to smuggling-related charges, he admitted to laundering more than $80-million U.S. *himself* during those six years. As the U.S. government continues their investigation into Miller's activities, each day they find more gaudy examples of wealth. Authorities are now seeking the forfeiture of more than $557-million U.S. in assets, including ten boats, five vans, five snowmobiles, more than a dozen pickup trucks, at least fifteen sport-utility vehicles, seventeen trailers, three Corvettes, five luxury cars, a coin collection, a tractor and eight properties. It is all owned by Miller and various other members of his ring.

CUSTOMS ACT, SECTIONS 159 & 160

Smuggling

159. Every person commits an offence who smuggles or attempts to smuggle into Canada, whether clandestinely or not, any goods subject to duties, or any goods the importation of which is prohibited, controlled or regulated by or pursuant to this or any other Act of Parliament.

Punishment

160. Every person who contravenes section 12, 13, 15, 16, subsection 20 (1), section 31 or 40, subsection 43 (2), 95 (1) or (3), 103 (3) or 107 (1) or section 153, 155, or 156 or commits an offence under section 159 or 159 (1)

(a) is guilty of an offence punishable on summary conviction and liable to a fine of not more than fifty thousand or to imprisonment for a term not exceeding six months or to both that fine and that imprisonment; or

(b) is guilty of an indictable offence and liable to a fine of not more than five hundred thousand dollars or to imprisonment for a term not exceeding five years or to both that fine and that imprisonment.

Miller's stature grew so large, he became to young smugglers what Bill Gates was to struggling computer programmers. Thousands wanted to emulate him and hundreds actually tried. The smugglers came to Cornwall the same way prospectors were lured to the Yukon during the gold rush a century ago.

One of the men who had been drawn in by the temptation of smuggling was Martino.

$ $ $

If Andre the Giant had a baby brother, it would be Martino.

He's the type of man for whom most doorways are too small, with arms bigger than other men's thighs and a broad back that seems strong enough to heft a piano. He even looks the part of the professional wrestler: a wild mane of shaggy black hair streaked with grey, a mangy goatee more silver than black, a grizzly bear's body, and eyes that make you want to cross the street to avoid him.

On this day, though, he looks small. He's folded himself onto a sofa in the living room of his Cornwall home and spends much of the afternoon clutching his head between his mammoth hands. On the big-screen television, the

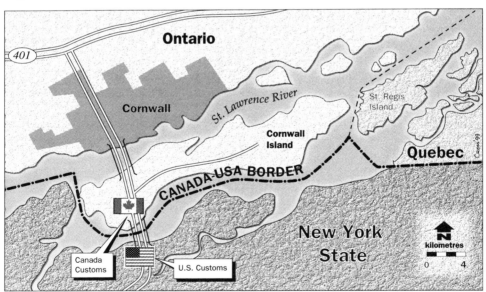

shopping channel makes its endless sales pitch. Martino is talking about how much money he's made through cigarette smuggling, how much money the police think he's made through cigarette smuggling, and finally, how much money he's lost because of his cigarette smuggling. It's a trying conversation for him.

"They say I made millions, I don't know what they're talking about," Martino says, rubbing his forehead. "After everything was paid out, I'd bring home between $2,000 and $3,500 a week if everything went right, and it didn't go right all the time, I'll tell you that much."

The government, not surprisingly, has a different opinion of Martino's activities. They say that at the height of his operation, he was responsible for smuggling $8-million worth of cigarettes across the border each week. The RCMP and Revenue Canada believe Martino and his partners defrauded the Canadian government of more than $100-million in taxes by smuggling tobacco and alcohol into Canada without paying duty. They call Martino "a kingpin."

Martino just laughs his gravelly laugh. "Was I in the cigarette business? Yeah. Everyone here was involved in cigarettes," Martino says, pointing out his living room window. "The police are calling me a kingpin, but if I was a kingpin, 90 per cent of the people in Cornwall were kingpins."

He rubs his face again and asks his wife to bring in some Pepsi's. Outside, there are kids riding their bicycles up and down the streets and Martino's two enormous German shepherds perk up their ears with each squeal of laughter and screech of tire.

Martino is filthy. He's been working all day with his horses; feeding them, grooming them, getting them their exercise. Ever since the government seized his stables and farm outside of town as part of the smuggling investigation, it's been difficult keeping the animals in shape. His stables had a wide gravel practice track for the horses to run on and acres of open space for them to graze. Now, he has to board the horses at a smaller farm and it's not the same quality of life for his animals or for him.

The constant trips to the farm weigh heavily on Martino. He's 43 and his body can't handle the physical work like it used to. When his wife returns with the Pepsi, he takes one, his hand dwarfing the green picnic glass. He rattles the ice inside and takes a long drink.

"You want to know how this all started? I'll tell you. I don't mind. It could have happened to anybody."

$ $ $

Cornwall was never home to Martino. He and his wife had lived in Toronto most of their lives, Martino having emigrated from Italy when he was a child and the wife having been born in the city. They met and fell in love when they were in their early 20s and got married in '76, a young couple bursting with dreams for the future.

It was a time of optimism. Toronto was going into a boom period then and a young man who was willing to work hard could make a fistful of money. Martino was such a young man, and he dedicated every waking hour to building a used car business.

After years of trudging out to every car auction and arranging financing for every poor soul who came into his lot, the business began to take off. He was making money on the cars, enough money to start to live some of those dreams. By the mid-1980s, Martino had enough money to move his wife to a beautiful home in Brampton, a suburb west of Toronto. They took some vacations and started to have enjoy their lives.

Martino even started to think about following his life-long ambition of owning a racehorse. His father had loved to bet horses and used to take Martino to the track as a child. It had been in his blood ever since. With all that money, life was fun.

Unfortunately for Martino, it became a little bit too fun. It was the '80s and for those with a certain amount of money and a certain amount of recklessness, cocaine was the style. Martino moved in circles where the drug was common and saw no reason not to dabble in it. Like so many others, for Martino that dabbling became regular use and that regular use became serious addiction. As the drugs took centre stage, everything else started to disintegrate. The used car business began to fail, the mortgage payments on the house in Brampton were no longer a priority, and home life lost most of its allure. His mind and body revolved around cocaine.

By the time Martino and his wife realized how serious the problem had become, it was too late. The business was faltering terribly, beyond the point of salvation. The mortgage was deep in arrears and there was no hope of catching up. Martino used the last of his dwindling resources to check himself into a drug rehab program. In 1989, he came out clean but penniless. He was forced to declare bankruptcy; everything he'd built was gone.

There were two ways to look at the situation: either it was a dead end or a fresh start. Martino chose the latter. Despite the setback he had the confidence of a man who had battled demons and won. If he could conquer cocaine, he could certainly win back his fortune.

He and his wife were sure of one thing: They wanted to get out of

Toronto. Too many old friends and bad memories in that city. The question was, where to go?

One day, Martino was talking to an old family friend in Cornwall. It sounded like a quaint spot. Located right on the St. Lawrence River, it was a busy little place with cheap houses and warm people. With the American border just minutes away, there were also plenty of opportunities for the industrious soul. Of course, out-of-towners sometimes made fun of Cornwall because the Domtar pulp and paper plant left the air smelling a little rank, but Martino's friend assured him it was something you got used to. And when you did, you had a beautiful waterfront playground with ample room for an ambitious man. If you have to start over, one place is as good as the next. Martino and his wife moved 250 miles east to Cornwall.

After he got his feet under him, Martino went back to what he knew best: used cars. He set up a new business right in downtown Cornwall and spent the first year building up contacts and scouring car lots and auctions for hidden gems that could make him a dollar. His business began to grow and as it did, he couldn't help but notice a lot of customers came in and paid cash for their cars. This was a definite change from Toronto and at first, a welcome

---

Other Illicit Cargo

Along with cigarettes, there's been drugs, guns, alcohol, and even freon gas smuggled between Canada and the United States through Cornwall and the St. Lawrence River area. But by far, the most dangerous, illicit cargo of all is humans.

The United States still shines as symbol of opportunity around the globe and people are willing to do just about anything to get there. That includes arriving in Canada, where security is more lax, and then getting smuggled across the border into their Promised Land. U.S. authorities estimate that more than 10,000 illegal aliens try to cross this section of the river every year. They arrive from all around the world, but China, Korea, and India tend to be the most common points of departure. Smugglers charge between $15,000 and $25,000 a head for this service, a high price considering it can sometimes have tragic results.

On Oct. 3, 1996, Naseem Taj, 51, and nine other refugee claimants from Pakistan were shuffled onto a boat in Cornwall with the promise they'd be delivered safely to the United States. But the rough waters of the St. Lawrence proved too much and the boat swamped. Taj drowned that night, and the man who smuggled her across is still before the court on manslaughter charges.

one. But as Martino worked to build a legitimate business, he slowly became aware of how much illegitimate business was being done in Cornwall.

The cash for cars was one sign. Then there always seemed to be more money around town than there should be. It didn't click at first. But when Martino started noticing that everywhere he went, people were offering to sell him cigarettes for $3 or $4 a pack, considerably less than they sold for in the corner stores and gas stations, it started to come together for him. Talking to people who came into his used car lot or chatting at the bar while out for an after-work beer, Martino slowly pieced together the economy of the illegal cigarette trade.

In the early '90s, cigarettes retailed at more than $40 for a carton of 200 cigarettes. When you bought by the pack, it cost you more than $5.50 to get your fix of Player's or du Maurier cigarettes. The catch was that most of that $40—between $22 and $24—was federal taxes. It wasn't only the pack-a-day smoker who was addicted to nicotine, but the revenue-hungry government as well. With the national debt soaring, finance ministers couldn't resist the urge to raise the so-called sin taxes, and each new budget added another quarter or so to the price of tobacco.

There was bound to be a breaking point, a point where the cost of cigarettes got so high consumers wouldn't tolerate it any more. That breaking point came just about the time Martino arrived in Cornwall.

The loophole was in Canada's own export laws. For Canadian cigarette manufacturers, the products they were exporting to other countries weren't subject to those high federal taxes. So a carton of Canadian cigarettes that cost $40 in Toronto could be bought for $16 to $18 wholesale in the United States, even after taking into account the more expensive American dollar.

It didn't take a financial wizard to see where money could be made in that equation. If cigarettes sold for $5.50 to $6 a pack in Canada, but you could buy the exact same pack for $2 to $2.25 in the United States, an entrepreneur could bring cheap cigarettes across the border and make a quick profit reselling them.

If you lived in Windsor and bought 20 cartons for $360 while on a day trip to Detroit, you could stash them in your trunk on the way home, forget to declare them at the border and then easily resell them for $500 or $600. For an area like Cornwall, where the United States lay just on the other side of the river and there was little to no border enforcement, it was ridiculously easy.

$ $ $

Those in the business called it "smuggler's paradise." Those with the RCMP called it "a chink in the armour." No matter how you looked at it, the waters off Cornwall were a nightmare for police and a dream for criminals.

It's only a two-minute boat ride across that part of the St. Lawrence, and there weren't many border patrols along that stretch. Then there was the scattering of islands between the U.S. side of the river and the Canadian side: Cornwall Island, St. Regis Island, Yellow Island, Cattle Island, Chatelain Island, Simard Island, and a dozen smaller ones. They provided perfect cover for a smuggler who was waiting to hop across the river in the dead of night. On the bridge, every car was subject to questioning by customs officials. There was no such rigorous checkpoint on the water. At night, smugglers could spot the lights of a patrol boat a kilometre away, so they simply waited until the river was dark and the coast was clear to make the run across.

The cartons of cigarettes bought for $16 to $18 in the States could be sold for between $25 and $30 each on the black market across the river—a quick profit of about $10 a carton. Considering you could easily fit 500 cartons of cigarettes in a small boat, that meant an entrepreneur could make $5,000 for a single trip across the St. Lawrence. For otherwise law-abiding citizens, it felt like the perfect crime.

The victim was neither a person or the most sympathetic figure. It was hard to feel guilty about short-changing the government a couple of dollars' worth of taxes by not paying the duty. They always seemed to get theirs anyway, what with the GST, the PST, the income tax, the liquor tax, the gas tax, and all the hidden tariffs.

Once one could rationalize the crime, one could also realize the risk of getting caught was minimal—customs couldn't search every car that crossed the bridge and it was impossible to monitor every boat that crossed the river. Even better, it wasn't like smuggling heroin or cocaine. In those cases, if any of the authorities as much as caught you with the product, you faced criminal

The Surrey-Miami Connection

While the Cornwall area remains a hot spot for smuggling, there's also brisk business being done at other points along the world's largest undefended border. There's one spot along the British Columbia-Washington State border, a little south of Surrey, that sees so many marijuana smugglers that the U.S. government's National Drug Control Policy office has labeled it as "a high-intensity" drug smuggling area—the same rating that Miami gets.

charges. With cigarettes, however, you could be sitting on the U.S. side of the river, loading 2,000 cartons into a boat in full view of the police and they could do nothing. It's not against the law to have cigarettes in your possession. It only becomes against the law when you transport them across the border. And since the border was in the middle of the river, the police were helpless when they came across smugglers preparing a load to run across the river. If you weren't caught in the act, you weren't caught.

Then, the punishment if you were caught was easy to swallow. If you were apprehended for just a single trip and police didn't have evidence of other smuggling, it was only the lightest of taps on the wrist. Either the cigarettes were confiscated or the smuggler was forced to pay duty on them. For the small-time operator, there was certainly no threat of jail hanging over any-body's head, no threat of one's family being embarrassed or expensive lawyers getting involved. It wasn't a crime of violence and the courts would have come to a standstill if every two-bit smuggler was taken before them.

To make cigarette smuggling all that more attractive, it was a product even the most unsavvy of people could unload. Unlike drugs or stolen prop-erty, where it might be difficult for the average citizen to find customers, there was no such problem with black market cigarettes. Everybody knew people who smoked, usually dozens or even hundreds of them. Small-time operators could move 50 or 100 cartons a week just through friends, family and co-workers.

Then, once you started branching out to people you knew in Ottawa, Toronto and Montreal, maybe hook up with a convenience store owner who wanted to increase his profit margin on cigarettes by buying cartons from you . . . it just went on and on. Cigarette manufacturers have gotten rich off the public's undying craving for nicotine, so the smugglers just followed the same beaten path to the smokers. Few people who smoke had such high moral standards that they refused to buy a black market pack of du Mauriers for $3.50 or $4, especially since most considered the product to be overtaxed to begin with. It was the righteous few who could turn their noses up at cheap cigarettes and walk down the street to the Mac's Milk and pay $6 on principle alone.

As Martino quickly learned that first year, in Cornwall most people either were in the cigarette business or knew somebody who was. The police were well aware of the abundance of smugglers but couldn't stop it because of the limited officers and other policing priorities. With the usual string of assaults, bank robberies and murders, police couldn't spare the time to crack down on what amounted to a tax violation.

"The smuggling business was booming in the early '90s in Cornwall," says Corp. Neil Foley, a veteran RCMP officer. "There wasn't a day that went by that you couldn't go up on the bridge between Cornwall and the U.S. and just watch boatloads of the cigarettes move across the river. It was just a wide-open, crazy time and it seemed every Tom, Dick and Harry was involved in some way."

Having lost everything he worked so hard for in Toronto to drugs and bankruptcy, Martino was eager to return to the lifestyle to which he had grown accustomed. Soon, he was just another Tom, Dick and Harry.

$ $ $

It's a line every young child uses after they've been caught smoking or throwing rocks through a school's windows or cheating on a history test: "Everybody else was doing it." It didn't yield much sympathy then and Martino knew it didn't garner any now either. But at least it was the truth, or for Martino, it appeared to be the truth.

From the vantage of his used car lot in downtown Cornwall, everybody seemed to be running cigarettes and getting rich off it. Every day another neighbour or friend or drinking buddy would be buying a new Jet-Ski or taking his wife on a trip to Mexico or lugging a brand new big-screen TV into their house. It was as if the money was waiting for him to grab it, mocking him for not having the courage to do so. How could he resist?

Sure enough, in 1991, Martino took a couple of trips across the river to scout out the situation, visit the cigarette wholesalers, and compare the prices. He discovered if you had the cash, the cigarettes were pretty much yours with few questions and fewer hassles.

Back in Cornwall, he began poking around to find out how the cigarettes were sold once they were brought over from the States. You need a network, Martino was told, people who want to buy them. There was no point in trying to sell them in Cornwall itself; that market had long since been saturated. That posed no problem. Martino had hundreds of old friends and business connections in Toronto from his days there. Many of them smoked, or knew people who did. At the very least, they all had a nose for money and realized that buying discount cigarettes was a great investment opportunity.

Martino made a couple of phone calls and confirmed that he would have no problem unloading hundreds, even thousands of cartons. The black market cigarette business was already substantial in Toronto and there was always a need for more, especially among convenience store and gas station owners who wanted to squeeze an extra dollar or two of profit out of a pack by buying smuggled cigarettes but selling them at retail prices.

Martino needed a partner for his enterprise, but for that he didn't have to look farther than his own house. He'd started renting out a room to a kid from Cornwall, a 22-year-old local who was always short of money and looking to make up the difference by any means possible. They bought a cheap boat and put together a stake of $3,200 to buy 200 cartons of cigarettes.

It was a cloudy afternoon when they drove over the bridge to the U.S. Martino and his young partner made the purchase, toting the cigarettes away in the back of a pick-up truck. After dark, they drove through the Akwesasne Reserve to the American edge of the St. Lawrence River. Under the cover of darkness, they loaded the cartons from the truck to the boat.

Martino got in the boat and with the running lights off, slowly crept out from shore, moving from one island to another, keeping in the shadows. His partner took the truck and drove across the bridge, paying the toll and clearing customs without a hitch. He drove to a prearranged spot on the Canadian side of the river where he would meet Martino. There was a stretch there of more than five miles that made for easy landing, a stretch too big to be policed and with enough nooks and crannies to hide a small boat.

Martino maneuvered the boat into shore and with blood pumping, they transferred the cigarettes back onto the pick-up truck. Martino drove them to Toronto that night and sold them for $5,000 to one of his buddies who ran another used car lot. He drove back to Cornwall the next afternoon, exhausted but $1,800 richer. Not bad for a day's work.

It wasn't hard for the businessman in Martino to start thinking on a bigger scale. If 200 cartons could net him $1,800, he could get a bigger boat and move 2,000 cartons and take home $18,000 . . . the possibilities seemed endless. Just look at Larry Miller and his Lear jet.

After that, Martino built the operation like he built his used car business, through hard work and networking. His friend in Toronto moved the first 200 cartons easily. He told Martino to bring down more any time. Through other friends, he had a contact in Montreal who was also hungry to get in on the business. The trips across the river became more frequent until they were an almost nightly event. Martino admits by 1993 he was moving as many as 8,000 cartons—between 300 and 400 cases of cigarettes—a week at a gross profit usually in the range of $8 a carton. Out of that he paid his partner, an accountant to help him hide the money, and drivers to move the cigarettes up and down Highway 401, to Montreal and Toronto where the bulk of the customers were.

For overseeing this operation, Martino says he earned about $3,500 a week during the peak years. It was a nice way to pad his income from the used car business and it helped fuel a seemingly luxurious lifestyle. He and his wife had a home in Cornwall, the stables outside of town, a condo in Florida, a nice boat, cars, and a motorcycle.

More important to Martino, the money let him pursue his love of horses. He began purchasing and training racehorses, running them at the track in Montreal on weekends. He slowly built up his stables until he had more than 30 horses, beautiful and strong animals all.

Looking around, Martino didn't think he was drawing much attention. It seemed every second car on the road was a brand new Jeep Cherokee or Corvette and the boat sales in Cornwall were going through the roof. The problem for Martino was that he peaked just when the authorities decided to crack down on smuggling. He was about to become a test case.

$ $ $

The competition among smugglers was now so intense that the area around Cornwall had truly become like the Wild West. High-speed boats were zipping back and forth across the river, gunfire was echoing over the water at night as rivals tried to scare each other off, and the smugglers would roll through the streets in their expensive cars, reeking of money. Those people in Cornwall and on the Akwesasne Territory who weren't in the business were genuinely tired of it all. They were demanding that police take action.

Meanwhile, the government realized it was losing hundreds of millions in tax revenue each year to the smugglers. They wanted to make an example of some people. The Americans were working on infiltrating the Larry Miller organization and the Canadians wanted a big fish of their own to fry. As the officers started to talk about potential targets, Martino's name came up. He was as good a candidate as any.

It was a joint investigation by the RCMP and Revenue Canada. The officers managed to get wiretaps on Martino's phones and began tracking his cigarette shipments. They fell into some real luck when they nabbed another man for a smuggling case and it turned out he was the one keeping Martino's books. In return for special consideration on his case, the rogue accountant agreed to roll over on Martino.

That gave the police exactly what they needed. Police ended up charging Martino with conspiracy to smuggle cigarettes and several proceeds-of-crime offences. The charges were dead serious; police documents show that they believed "the Martino organization" smuggled 4,000 cases of cigarettes—a street value of $8-million—into Canada every week.

But the charges didn't impress Martino and neither did the police figures. He calls the $8-million estimate a joke. He calls the whole operation a joke.

"Why me? They could've hit anybody, but they hit me," he says, still honestly puzzled by the charges. "I didn't do nothing that everybody else wasn't doing."

Nonetheless, in March 1998, Martino ended up pleading guilty to the charges. He says he wanted to fight them, but agreed to the plea bargain only because the police had charged his wife with conspiracy to smuggle as well.

"They said they were going to put her in jail. I couldn't live with that, so I agreed to plead guilty," he explains. "That way, they dropped the charges against my wife."

Martino got hit with an 18-month conditional jail sentence. That sentence meant he would never have to spend a day in jail so long as he kept to such conditions as abstaining from alcohol and not committing any other criminal acts.

What was worse for Martino were the proceeds-of-crime investigators who swooped down on him. On the original indictments, police set out a range of items they hoped to seize. Prime among them were the stables and home outside of Cornwall, several other Cornwall-area properties, a condo in Pompano Beach, Florida, more than $260,000 in cash, several cars, and a boat. Martino was allowed to keep his horses because as a rule, the police and government didn't like to seize anything that ate; too much trouble to keep animals fed and exercised.

Even after he gave his guilty plea and his assets were stripped away, it wasn't over for Martino. The government vultures were fighting over the stables outside of Cornwall. Both Revenue Canada and the federal Crown's office wanted them, the former to pay for back taxes, the latter to cover the cost of the investigation. In the end, the two branches of government went to court to fight it out over the last shred of Martino's cigarette smuggling legacy.

That decision was handed down in December 1998. Justice Robert Desmarais ruled that Martino's farm and stables should be classified as proceeds of crime and would be kept by the Crown. Even the judge saw the situation as slightly absurd, calling the motion by Revenue Canada to seize the stables "the robbing of Paul to pay Peter."

It didn't matter to Martino. They were never going to be returned to him. Nine months after pleading guilty to the charges, Martino was putting his life back together one piece at a time. He was never a bad man; a man who gave into temptation, yes, but never bad. He still had his wife, he still had a place to live in Cornwall and he still had his horses. He spent most of his days with them, preparing them for races in Montreal where they ran for purses of a couple thousand dollars. Sometimes they won; more often than not they lost. But it was still enough money to keep the family going.

The salad days of cigarette smuggling are over in Cornwall. The government finally showed the wisdom to drop tobacco taxes enough to cut the juicy profit out of the smuggling trade. The most that can be made now is $4 or $5 a carton, nowhere near enough incentive to draw in the little guys, the mom-and-pop smuggling organizations. Now the only way to make money is through volume smuggling, and only organized crime groups can handle that. While five years ago there were hundreds of smugglers on the river, now there are just a handful of professional groups. The problem isn't entirely gone, and what remains is a little more complex.

Walking out of court that December day, preparing to face the icy drive from Ottawa back down to Cornwall, Martino was philosophical about his smuggling days. In the end, he was right back where he started when he had first come to Cornwall a decade before.

"I guess we'll see what happens now," Martino said. "It's all gone now. Everything. It was all money for nothing."

IN OVER HIS HEAD:
A CAR THIEF GETS JAMMED UP

There's a freaked-out man on the wrong end of a manic swing on my couch who nearly bit off the finger of a fellow driver over a minor traffic dispute seven hours ago and he's hiding out in my apartment because the police sent a SWAT team and a canine unit after him because when witnesses called 911 to report the fight they gave the operator his licence plate number and his name came up on the computer as Code 64—USE EXTREME CAU-TION—thanks to the fact that he has a criminal record with something like 90 hits on it including assaulting a police officer but even with the cops and the dogs swarming after him he got away by driving across a baseball diamond in his shiny black GMC truck with three scanners going to keep track of the police pursuit and a two-four of Export in the back and a hunting knife on the seat beside him and now he's here in my apartment with my old friend from high school Mike Barnett and it's 1:52 a.m. and we're just kind of trying to figure out what to do half expecting the police to break down the door any damn minute.

Deep breath.

Okay. Here's what happened.

Remember the Alonzo Mendez investigation?

You know the one—that crazy businessman who makes a tidy living by launching a thousand nuisance suits and living off the proceeds. He looks like a million bucks with his expensive Italian suits and silver hair and beautiful blonde wife, but if you talk to him for five minutes you quickly realize he's a little delusional and borderline psychotic.

That's where the whole story starts.

Remember how Mendez got screwed royally by a bunch of his former business partners back in 1992? He lost about $180,000 in total on a land venture that supposedly went bad, but he suspects it ended up lining his partners' pockets. He went after them with a civil suit (surprise surprise) but they got it thrown out of court in 1996. He's been looking for revenge ever since.

Last year, Mendez started up a private investigation company—his latest business venture—and he came up with a plan to blackmail the guys who he thinks fucked him.

Here's what he sets out to do: He's going to hire hookers to pose as businesswomen or potential clients and have them visit the offices of his former partners to try to lure them back to hotel rooms or apartments that are completely rigged with video cameras and sound mikes. Mendez's plan is to catch them in the carnal act, get the video and audio evidence, and then confront them: "You don't want your wife to know? You don't want the community to know? Then give me the $180,000 you stole from me."

This plan might be a problem anytime but it's a *fucking* wasps' nest when it turns out the two men Mendez is trying to set up are Lionel Briggs, the rich husband of that retired Liberal Member of Parliament, and Stuart Hughes, the millionaire accountant who owns a bunch of bars and real estate downtown.

Here's where my old friend Mike Barnett comes into the picture. Remember him? Skinny guy, dark hair, can't get enough of '80s rock? He's the sweetest man in the world, but somehow trouble always seems to find him.

Back in December 1997, Mike was fresh from private investigation school, one of those courses you see advertised on the back of matchbooks or on late-night TV. You drop $2,700 on a three-month program and then you're qualified. It sounds more romantic than it is. He took the course and got the regular run of shitty jobs you'd expect it would yield: following husbands on the make, floor-walking at department stores during Christmas—that kind of stuff. It's all spotty work and not very profitable, so when an ad appears in the newspaper the first week of January 1998 saying a new company, Triumph Investigative Services, is hiring private investigators, he goes in for an interview.

It's Alonzo Mendez's baby, of course. Mendez sits there with his Hugo Boss suit and slick smile, acting smooth as hell. He's talking about a new era in investigative services, talking about the vast fortunes to be made, talking about profit sharing. Mike is hooked. He reports to work the next day.

The first couple of shifts are routine, a bit of surveillance work, helping set up the office, that sort of thing. But a couple of weeks later, Mendez wants to send Mike out on a special job. It's an insurance sting, he explains.

Mendez says this banking executive is bilking an insurance company and Triumph has been hired to get it on tape. Mike's job is to accompany a fellow operative—a young woman named Laney—to the man's office. Since he's a bank manager, they're going to pose as a young married couple looking for a loan. Mike and Laney are supposed to pretend to get in a fight in his office and Mike's going to storm out, yelling about the marriage being over and she's nothing but a lousy bitch. The girl's going to get the statement after that, Mendez says.

In the car ride over, Mike and Laney start to talk. It's the first time they've met.

"I'm nervous. I don't like doing this," she says to Mike.

"I know, it's scary, but it's kind of fun. It's like acting," Mike says. "It'll be all right."

Then Laney starts crying. "I don't want to do this."

"What? It's not that bad. It'll be all right, really. What's wrong?"

She cries more, not wanting to say, but eventually she tells him.

It's her job to sleep with him, sleep with the bank manager. After Mike storms out, she's supposed to break down and cry and ask to be held and then tell the manager she really needs a drink and would he go with her? Just for company of course, just for somebody to talk to. After the drinks, Laney has to act flirtatious and vulnerable and lure him back to an apartment where the hidden video camera's all set up and ready to start rolling.

Mike stops the car when he hears this. He doesn't know what to do.

Theft: The Legalities

CANADIAN CRIMINAL CODE, SECTION 334

Except where otherwise provided by law, everyone who commits theft

  (a) is guilty of an indictable offence and liable to imprisonment for a term not exceeding ten years where the property stolen is a testamentary instrument or the value of what is stolen exceeds five thousand dollars

  (b) is guilty

  (i) of an indictable offence and is liable to a term of imprisonment not exceeding two years, or

  (ii) if an offence punishable on summary conviction where the value of what is stolen does not exceed five thousand dollars

This is not right, he tells himself. This is scary shit.

He decides right then that he's not going to play this game. He turns the car around and takes Laney home. They talk more. She's young, 18, 19, and she's already slept with Mendez and she has a baby inside her that needs to be aborted. At least it's not from him, thank God, that lousy prick who's old enough to be her grandfather, because he just fucked her two weeks ago for the first time.

"We've got to get you out of here. Where can you go?" Mike asks.

She has relatives out of town and they always told Laney to call anytime. This is the time. She's staying at a dive motel in the east end, so they pack up her stuff and he drives her 45 minutes away to where her aunt and uncle live.

Mike's out of his mind driving back to the Triumph offices, but he doesn't let on. He needs the job too much, he needs the paycheque because, damn, he's just been married five months, he's almost 30, and he hasn't brought home a regular, decent cheque in close to two years. He already owes $12,000 to his dad for the P.I. course and he can't face hitting the classified ads again. As long as he doesn't have to cross the line, he tells himself, he'll stick this thing out a little bit longer.

So he goes back to Triumph, tells Mendez that Laney lost it and ran away when they pulled into the bank parking lot. Mendez just grunts and Mike says nothing more. That was the third week of January.

A little bit later, in early March now, he's coming into the office, doing some routine insurance work for Mendez this time. You know, a guy has an accident at work, goes off on long-term disability and then proceeds to pump iron at the gym, wrestle with his son and build a new deck at the cottage—all the things a severely injured man shouldn't be able to do.

So Mike follows him to a batting cage, gets right up beside him with a harmless-looking duffel bag in his hand. He sits down at a picnic table, puts the duffel bag beside him, and watches as the guy stretches then steps into the cage. For the next 30 minutes, he hammers away at 70-mile-per-hour fastballs, sending the balls screaming against the black netting at the rear of the cage.

Not bad for a guy with such a bad back he can't work.

It's all caught on tape, on an efficient little remote machine hidden in the side of the duffel bag that beams the damaging evidence to a surveillance truck outside. That's the kind of footage that makes insurance execs giddy with delight.

That day, Mike's in the office typing up the final report on the operation to submit with the batting cage videotape. When he's done he walks into the photocopy room, wanting to make a copy for him and one for the company files. He lifts the lid on the photocopier and there he sees a small, white, square piece of paper. It's the back of a photograph. Mike turns it over and it's a picture of a man getting a blow job from one damn ugly woman.

Mike is stunned. He walks into Mendez's office to ask what the hell is going on now. Mendez is sitting at the desk with a pair of white plastic gloves on. Using a pair of tweezers, he's inserting a photocopy of the picture into an envelope. The envelope is addressed to Stuart Hughes. Hughes, of course, is the millionaire accountant and real estate tycoon who allegedly helped defraud Mendez of that $180,000. Mike thinks Hughes looks far too much like Nick, Carla's ex-husband on *Cheers*, the one who scores the Amazon blonde goddess much to the shock and dismay of Carla.

"Now's not a good time Mike," is all Mendez says.

Mike swirls in the doorway, a quick 180, back to the photocopy room where he replaces the picture on the surface of the machine and closes the lid. What the hell is he going to do now? First the girl at the bank, now this. Something is going on. He needs a cigarette so bad his lungs are contracting inside his chest.

He steps out into the parking lot and with a shaky hand lights a du Maurier. Just then, Josh pulls up in his hot black GMC Jimmy.

Josh is an electronics genius. He's the one who built the camera into the duffel bag that Mike used to nail the guy at the batting cage. He was a great guy, real solid, and from what Mike knew, he had a good street rep too. They'd started talking when they were planning the duffel bag job and quickly became friends. In a tie and long sleeves, Josh looked clean cut and harmless, but Mike had soon learned that that was just a front.

From the time Josh was 12, he was picking locks and causing trouble. He started out with the lock on his dad's filing cabinet then moved on to the deadbolt on the front door. After that, it was locks at school, at friends' houses, wherever. Each new lock was like a new puzzle that Josh relished finishing. By the time he was 14, he could get into a house in less than 60 seconds with just a safety pin and a paper clip.

Break-and-enters seemed natural considering his skills, though at first he just broke, entered and left. The thrill was getting inside, not taking shit. But when he told his friends about his deeds, they thought he was insane for not stealing anything. They kept on asking what he got when he went in, so after a while, he just started getting.

When he was 16, he and his buddies broke into the Sears outlet, stole more than 75 VCRs and other assorted merchandise. While in the store, Josh picked out special equipment for himself, high-end gear that would help with his growing fascination with electronics. He put red stickers on the items he wanted so his crew wouldn't grab them or put them with the stuff that was going to be fenced the next day.

After the job, they drove back to Josh's dad's place to unload. As it happened, his dad had company over, a couple of women he was trying to get a leg over on, so he didn't really notice all the traffic into the basement through the back door. When they were almost done unloading, Josh's dad started to get suspicious, what with all the noise, so he went to investigate. He came down to the basement and saw a stack of VCRs, all types, all brands. He turned to Josh.

"Which one's mine?"

Josh laughed and his dad picked one up. It was the one with the red fucking sticker on it.

"Fuck, Dad, you can't have that one. Any other one but that!"

"Jesus Christ, son, I'm your father." He cursed out Josh for a few minutes, then grabbed a VCR and a Sony Handi-Cam and went back upstairs.

A couple of months later, his dad was still hassling him for stuff. Josh came back one morning, about 3 a.m. with a set of silk sheets and pillowcases. His dad wanted them.

"Dad, just go back to the store. The fucking door's still open."

A month later he was out, moving in with this Henry guy, a real piece of work but better than his father. When Henry and Josh went down for a series of break-and-enters a year-and-a-half later, the cops arrested them at their apartment. Josh had swiped a Neighbourhood Watch sign the year before and they had it hanging on the living-room wall. That got a laugh from the cops.

After being convicted, Josh went in front of Judge Gallagher, a self-righteous fuck at the best of times.

"Eighteen-, nineteen-year-olds are flying fighter planes in wars and raising families. They are men in their societies. Look at you: You are wasting your life. You have to be responsible for your actions," Gallagher told him.

Josh got hit with an 18-month sentence, a damn hard knock for a guy with no prior record. He had just turned 19.

At least they shipped him to a low-security joint for non-violents outside of Kingston. He had his own room with a key, took classes during the day, and was even allowed to pursue electronics as a hobby. One week he broke down one of the payphones at the prison and rigged it for unlimited long-distance calls—Vietnam, Lebanon, Vancouver, Montreal, whatever. He charged other inmates five bucks a call, all you could talk. You can bet this made him pretty popular on the inside.

His lock-picking skills also came in handy. He got so adept that he could pick the lock to his own prison room and change the cylinder so his key worked and the guard's didn't. He had 18 months to serve. He was bored. What else was there to do?

After he gets out of Frontenac, he's an even bigger nightmare. More break-and-enters, more dumb-ass jobs. Anything for money. One time he and his buddy are robbing a MoneyMart, no weapons, just notes. The cops come in, take down his partner. Another officer grabs Josh around the neck from behind and is just choking the hell out of him, trying to subdue him. Josh tries a backward snap kick to the cop's balls, but no use.

Then Josh pulls out an aerosol can of military-grade tear gas and sprays a jet of that corrosive shit right down the cop's throat. A tap on the can and it's a mist, press down hard on the button and it's a steady stream. Josh is jamming that button hard and that stream is pouring into the cop's eyes and mouth. The tear gas is so strong that the stuff is bouncing back and hitting Josh in the neck and that's burning the hell out of Josh's skin.

He's pinched for that of course. The arresting officers give Josh the sound shit kicking he deserves in the back of the cruiser and a couple of months later he gets convicted of assault police and robbery. The officer ends up with severe throat burns and temporary blindness. Josh ends up back in jail.

Thing is though, Josh straightens out after that. He gets out of jail in 1993 and he's 23 now. His criminal record is longer than his arm and he's tired of the hassles. It helps that he just met a wonderful woman who knows about his past and wants to support him. He ends up moving in with her, getting married, working odd jobs, concentrating on his love for electronics and high-tech surveillance equipment. He sort of drifts for five years, breaking no laws but not really doing much good either.

Then, in January 1998, about the same time Mike and Laney are driving to meet the bank manager, Josh is at the Bleeker electronics store, picking up a new scanner he'd ordered the month before. He can't help it. He teases the poor clerk behind the counter.

"You know what this is?" he asks.

Of course not.

Josh runs through the specs: it can intercept cordless phone calls, cellular phone calls, phone-banking systems, the works. Better yet, it's smaller than a deck of cards. Josh gives a quick demonstration. The clerk whistles through his teeth, impressed at the scanner and Josh's graphic descriptions of what it can do.

"You know, there was some guy in here last week. He left his card . . ." The clerk fishes behind the counter and pulls it out. "Triumph Investigative Services, that's it. Some guy was in here looking at equipment. He was asking if we knew anybody who did this kind of stuff. We said no, but I said I'd keep an eye out. He said there was some good money in it. Do you want me to call him?"

Josh was thrilled with the idea. Somebody into the same high-tech equipment, somebody with serious money, and maybe a real job to offer. Josh gave the clerk his pager number. He'd been out of the store 15 minutes when he got the beep from Mendez. He agreed to meet at the headquarters of Triumph later that afternoon.

"So, you have a criminal record?"

That was the first thing Mendez asked him. The question pissed off Josh, but it made Mendez happy when he nodded his head. After a little talk about surveillance and what Josh could do with locks, he was hired.

He had been working for Mendez for a month when Mike joined the firm. Josh and Mike gravitated towards each other. They were both smokers, so they took cigarette breaks together and they got to know each other better when Mendez teamed them up on a couple of surveillance jobs together. They wired up cameras, they intercepted phone calls, they rigged up the duffel bag. It was like being a spy and they both loved it.

When Mike saw the photograph of Stuart Hughes getting head from the ugly woman, it was Josh he wanted to talk to.

Mike's coming out of the building for a cigarette when Josh pulls into the parking lot. Mike goes up to his truck.

"We need to talk. Let's go for a drive."

They talk garbage for 20 minutes, testing the waters with each other.

"Have you seen anything weird around here?" Mike finally asks.

Josh thinks about the question, then nods.

"I don't think this is a good situation here," Mike says.

Josh nods again. It wasn't good. "What'd ya see?" he asks Mike.

Mike launches into the story of the bank manager and the girl with the baby in her stomach and then goes right into the picture of the guy getting head he found on the photocopier. Josh nearly busts a gut laughing when Mike describes Mendez hunched over at his desk with the tweezers, putting the picture into the envelope.

"Wait till you hear this," says Josh, wiping tears from his eyes.

A couple of weeks ago, Mendez asked Josh if he could do a special job. Lionel Briggs. The name had rung a vague bell in Josh's head. Mendez told him about Briggs' real estate empire and his high-profile wife.

"That thief stole $180,000 from me. I know it and I can prove it, I just need your help," Mendez told Josh.

The first thing he asked Josh to do was follow Briggs 16 hours a day. One day, Josh tracked Briggs to his girlfriend's place in the south end of the city. When he reported that to Mendez, Josh had to go by the girlfriend's place every afternoon and roller-blade endlessly around the block, waiting for the two to meet again so he could capture their magic moment on videotape. He got the footage.

After that job, Mendez came to him with another request. He knew about Josh's break-and-enters, he knew about his way with locks, he knew about his cameras.

Can you break into Briggs' house? Mendez asked. Can you put an intercept on his phone, wire up the house with mikes and put a couple of video cameras in the bedroom? And while you're at it, can you root around in the study and see if you can find any confirmation numbers of offshore bank accounts?

Josh was floored.

"Well, can you do it? I need your help on this one," Mendez said.

"Yeah, yeah," Josh said, buying time. "I'll get on it."

He did nothing for a week, not wanting to touch this one. Mendez came to him again to ask if the job had been done. No, not yet, said Josh.

"Can't you do it?" Mendez asked. "I thought you were good. If you can't do it, tell me. I'll get somebody else."

"I'll get on it," said Josh, swallowing hard at Mendez's sinister tone.

That was last week. Now he's talking to Mike in the truck.

The two sit in silence and digest each other's stories. This was heavy. Something is definitely wrong with this company. Thing is, they both need the paycheques. What to do? They decide they need advice. That's when I come into the story.

For whatever reason, Mike remembers me, his old friend from high school who now happens to report on crime for a major daily newspaper. It's the middle of March when he calls me and I agree to meet him that night at Tramps. That's when I hear the whole story.

"What should I do?" Mike asks me.

The whole thing throws me for a loop. I happened to have gone snow-boarding for the first time that day and I'm aching from head to toe because I fell on my face so many damn times. Now I have a couple of beers in me and I'm feeling a tad drunk and I hear this absurd tale that sounds like the plot from an Elmore Leonard novel. But Mike's my friend, and damn, the story would be hot. So I lay some advice on him.

"Stick in there for a while," I tell him. "Just don't do anything illegal. You can't quit, you need the money. You've got a wife, you've got rent to pay. Besides, you've done nothing wrong. Sit on it. If it goes bad, real bad, then you can tell the police. For now, just ride it out, keep an eye on things."

"Yeah, that's what I been thinking," says Mike. "I been writing stuff down, eh? Just in case."

So Mike sticks it out at Triumph Investigative Services and I try to look into the story. It's surreal, too surreal. I almost don't believe it. I make some checks at the cop shop, but none of the detectives know what I'm talking about. I wait.

Then, three months later, in June 1998, I catch a break. Out of the blue. An anonymous letter:

> Alonzo Mendez, The president of Triumph Investigative Services, is under investigation by both The Ottawa Carleton Regional Police and The RCMP for extortion. It's a high-profile investigation and There will be charges. I advise you To look into This.
>
> A Concerned Citizen

The letter is sent to everybody—TV, radio, the newspapers. By chance, it lands on my desk.

To everybody else, it's a quack, or even if they think it's true, it's unverifiable—no names of investigating officers, no names of victims, nothing solid to go on.

Not for me. I'm pretty sure I know where the letter's coming from. If Briggs and Hughes are being tailed by Mendez, they'd find out sooner or later and they'd want to counter-attack. With their money and Briggs' high-profile wife, they have the resources to fight back hard. They've probably complained to police and now want the media involved to publicly embarrass their old nemesis.

I call Mike this time and we meet at Tramps again.

When I tell him about the letter, Mike gets nervous. If the police come in, he could get nailed. I tell him I'll look into this, see how far the investigation is going. I jot down some names and dates Mike gives me, including that of Stuart Hughes. He was the guy caught on camera getting head.

That week, I go to the accountant to try and get to the bottom of this. Hughes confirms he's the one who called the police. He tells me he received a picture in the mail of him in a compromising situation and took it as a blackmail attempt. Hughes gives me the names of two cops.

The first name is a detective from the general assignment division, the guy who took the initial call from Hughes. This detective looked into it, but his gut instinct was that Hughes was a bit of a nutcase himself and the case looked impossible to prove. Since the cop had casework coming out his ass, he let it drop.

The investigation ends there, right? Not a chance. A call is placed to police after Hughes is told the investigation is over. Senior police officials are told to make the Mendez investigation a priority. Where does the call come from? We don't know. Who makes it? Somebody from the RCMP, way high up. Why? My guess is Briggs got his wife to pull some strings. She packs that kind of punch.

So the police re-open the case and assign it to one of their very top major crime investigators, one Det. Stephen Lang. He has one of the force's top clearance rates and handles only the biggest cases. Remember the gang killings three years ago? That was his. So were the drug killings last year. This is the second name the accountant Hughes gave me.

"He's looking into it now," Hughes told me with a wink.

This is a stroke of luck. I know Lang pretty well from covering murders and drinking down at the police club. I drive right over to his office at police headquarters for an off-the-record chat.

"How the hell do you know all that?" he says after he closed the door and heard me out.

He was shocked. How did I even know about the case? How did I know so much about the case? How did I know more about the case than Lang does?

I tell him a bit, about my friend on the inside, just enough to let him understand the situation. I don't want to play all my cards yet. We end up talking for a couple of hours. I get a great deal from Lang.

He's desperate to get a move on this case. The pressure is coming from the chief. Whoever called in to complain after the case was initially dropped has enough weight to make people jumpy. Lang needs my help, or more specifically, the help of my as-of-yet-unnamed friend who is on the inside of this Mendez debacle. Here's the deal: I get the exclusive story when it breaks, all the inside information. My buddy Mike gets complete protection from any charges that might drop. All I have to do is persuade Mike to tell Lang everything he's told me.

I meet Mike later that week. He's so tense and scared, it's easy to convince him to like the deal.

The investigation goes, goes hard with Mike on board. More names, more leads, more access to files. It takes more than eight months of work, but charges are finally laid against Mendez in early 1999. The case was all over the front page, considering the big names involved. Mendez ends up behind the eight ball, I end up with the juicy scoop and my old friend Mike has become the nearest and dearest friend of some very senior police officials.

Fast forward to May 1999. I'm doing my book on criminals and I want to do a chapter on car thieves. Josh, Mike's old pal from Triumph, is the best I've met. He started out doing it for the joy rides as a 13-year-old but then he started doing it for profit, to support his electronics habit. It was such easy work. He took an order for a Mercedes or a BMW, located the right vehicle, popped the locks and hot-wired the car. A quick drive to Montreal and he got $500 cash plus a train ticket home. He hasn't pulled one of these jobs since he went straight, but I figure he'll have more than enough stories to fill a couple of pages.

He's an ideal candidate too because he's such a decent guy. I've been out to dinner with him before and had him over to my apartment. Despite his past, I'd trust him with anything. For that, he always teases me about how naïve I am. If I don't put the chain lock on my apartment door, he'll grab a pin and a paperclip and open my deadbolt in 40 seconds.

"See how easy it is?" he tells me. "You have to protect yourself."

Every time I use my cordless phone, he'll flip out on me.

"Anybody could be listening in on that. Anybody!" he chides me.

Once, to prove his point, he whipped out his $900 pocket digital scanner while I was on the phone with my girlfriend. Within a couple of minutes I heard a strange echo. He was listening to every word on his scanner.

I tend to use my chain and be careful of what I say on the phone since I met Josh.

When I called him and asked him to help me out on my book, he was enthusiastic.

"I'd love to talk man," he tells me over the phone. "You should do a whole chapter on me, I'm a product. They stick me in jail at 19 for a first offence! They say I did 50 break-and-enters—well, 48 of them were in the same damn mall! They were right next to each other. That's not 48, that's one! I should've never gone to jail. I absorbed so much in there. I'm a product of society. The government shouldn't have put me there."

Happy to have such a talkative source, I invite Josh over the next evening.

The next afternoon, three hours before he's supposed to be at my place, it all hits the fan.

He's driving with a buddy, going to pick up hamburgers. Josh is depressed and angry, has been all week. First, this Alonzo Mendez shit has been all over the newspapers, fucking with his income. He's already been questioned by police and that's stressing him out, even though Mike made Lang promise Josh wouldn't be charged. But it's all getting to him. It kicks his manic side into gear.

Then it turns out this bullshit is the final straw for his wife. After all these years of crime, turbulence and night-time surveillance operations with Triumph, she's had it. She supported him when he got out of jail, she supported him all those years when he was going straight, and she supported him when he started at Triumph. But she's a good girl and she's had enough. She wants to date somebody normal. She wants out of the marriage. She loves Josh but she can't take him any more. She told him earlier that week.

Josh was half expecting it but he's still hurt. So he's out with his buddy, talking, trying to blow off steam. They're heading to McDonald's for hamburgers.

That's when some motherfucker comes speeding up behind him in a shitty old Ford LTD. Josh is going 60 and this guy comes up at about 110, the car just blowing up onto Josh's tail. For some reason, that pisses Josh right off. He taps the brakes hard, for no reason at all, just so his brake lights startle the crap out of the prick behind him.

It works. The guy slams on his

CAR THEFTS IN CANADA

Most Stolen

1. Acura Integra (2dr)
2. Honda Prelude (2dr)
3. Jeep TJ (2dr, 4WD)
4. Jeep Grand Cherokee (4dr, 4WD)
5. Dodge Ram 3500 pickup (4WD)
6. Acura Integra (4dr)
7. Jeep Cherokee (4dr, 4WD)
8. BMW 328i (2dr)
9. Chevrolet Cavalier Z24
10. Ford Mustang GT

Least Stolen

1. Buick Park Avenue
2. Mercury Grand Marquis
3. Buick LeSabre
4. Oldsmobile Eighty-eight
5. Buick Skylark
6. Chevrolet Lumina
7. Lincoln Town Car
8. Chrysler Concorde
9. Buick Regal
10. Buick Century

(Source: Vehicle Information Centre of Canada, 1996–97 data)

own brakes, screeching a bit. Then he swings out and pulls his LTD beside Josh. They're both doing about 45 now.

"You fucking motherfucking piece of shit!" the guy screams out the passenger window, shaking his fist and thrusting his finger at Josh. Josh returns the message and then some.

The guy speeds ahead and pulls right in front of Josh, stopping quick to cut him off.

Josh is driving his beautiful, fully loaded black 1997 GMC Jimmy, complete with tinted windows. He has three police scanners mounted on the dash for his work with Triumph and a case of beer in the back. For some reason, Josh has a hunting knife with him, lying on the front seat in plain view. Josh can stop in time if he really tries. He doesn't give one fuck.

He hits the brakes but gives the shitbag's car a nice little smash, crumpling in the rear bumper. They're both out of their cars in a flash, the prick running at Josh. Out of the blue, he swings hard, catching Josh right where the top of his nose meets his eyebrow. He's screeching, at the top of his lungs.

"MY DAD DIED YESTERDAY! MY FUCKING DAD DIED YESTERDAY! MY FUCKING DAD DIED YESTERDAY!"

He keeps swinging and screaming, tears pouring down his cheek. He hits Josh in the nose this time, giving it a good crack. Then he grabs Josh in a side-headlock and tries to inflict more damage.

This is a bad idea.

Josh is now very mad and ready to fight. And Josh knows martial arts, even has the Asian tattoos on his thighs and forearms.

Josh takes the guy's pinky finger in his mouth and just bites, as hard as he can. He doesn't feel the finger come off in his mouth, but he felt his teeth against bone and blood gush into his mouth. That loosens the guy's headlock enough.

Josh stands up straight and gives the prick a backwards snap kick. The guy's right behind him so he just hops off his left foot and kicks his right leg backward, swinging hard at the knee and driving his heel into the guy's testicles. He lets go of Josh after that, but Josh is not done.

Moving away from him now, his back still to the other man, Josh swings his left hand backwards, fist closed. The back punch messes up the side of the guy's face and hurts Josh's hand pretty good too. He doesn't feel it now, but it'll hurt like hell in three hours.

Josh turns now, facing his opponent for the first time since he got surprised by the volley of punches. He kicks him hard, right to the side of the face. His white sandal comes off and goes skidding a couple yards down the street. The man drops to the ground, clutching his nose.

"I gave him some serious Van Damme-age," Josh says later. The sirens are audible now, in the distance. There's a crowd of about 30 people watching the fight. One of the women spotted the knife in the truck. Another guy with a cell called 911.

Josh hops in and drives, all scanners tuned to police frequencies. He's blocks away when the first squad cars get to the scene. His buddy with the burgers, he's still there and gets grabbed up. The cops run the licence plate and pull up Josh's name on the police computer. There are those damn 90 hits on his criminal record.

"But that's everything, they don't wipe off the ones that get dropped. Every time you get charged, it's all on there. They keep everything," Josh told me by way of explanation.

After Josh's name came up, there was the warning—CODE 64: USE EXTREME CAUTION—he had sprayed military tear gas down a cop's throat, don't forget. When the cops realize just who Josh is, they go on high alert. They send for the tactical and the canine units. Within five minutes, dogs and SWAT team members are combing the scene. When the woman who saw the knife tells this to police, that goes out over the scanner too. He's dangerous and he's armed with a knife.

"It was like *First Blood* out there, they just sent everybody after me. I was like Rambo, I just wanted to go home," Josh says.

Luckily, he's long gone by then, having cut across a baseball diamond and into a maze of side streets. He ditches the truck and calls his pal Mike Barnett for a ride *and* a hide.

Mike calls me on his cell.

"You still want to do that interview with Josh?"

Of course, I say. I know nothing about the carnage that has just transpired.

"You won't believe this," Mike continues. "We'll be right over."

They want drugs of course. It's not that Josh wasn't wanting to talk to me. He was even excited about it, remember? But when there's an all-points-bulletin out for him and what could be aggravated assault charges hanging over his head, I honestly don't think Josh's first priority is to keep his appointment with me and chat about his life. They're coming over because I keep a small cache of high-grade marijuana in my freezer for just such occasions. Josh needs to settle down.

After they come in, I sit for an hour, mesmerized, just listening to the day's events.

"My sandal just flew off, I have one sandal," he says after finishing the story. "It was on the road, they must have picked it up. It was white. They retained my sandal. They *retained* it! Fuck. I'm going to have to *retain* a lawyer tomorrow!"

That breaks the mood. We're all laughing now. At least Josh has a sense of humour. He opens up to the laughter.

"I didn't even get to eat my burger, man. I left that behind too. It went cold."

So we talk and smoke, smoke and talk. We need to come up with a plan. It's sometime after midnight when we finally arrive at one.

Mike is already helping out the police, but only as an informant. He never wanted his name to come out and he never wanted to have to testify against Mendez. The thing is, lately Mike's been getting pressure from Lang to come on board and testify. And part of Mike feels obligated to. Mendez is trouble and he needs to be taken down.

I remember talking to Detective Lang just last month, at a hockey game. He bought me a beer, thanking me again for hooking him up with Mike. I thanked him for keeping his side of the deal and giving me the exclusive story.

At that point, Mike was still on the fence as to whether he should become an on-the-record witness. That day at the hockey game, Lang tells me they have Mendez pretty good but with his money and lawyers, he might be able to squeeze out of it.

"Boy, jeez, if we had Mike on board, we'd close it for sure," he says, working me as we drink more beer. "He's a good kid, he's as straight as they come. Him in front of a jury? Jeez, that'd pretty much seal it."

Since then, Mike had talked to Lang and had pretty much agreed to testify on the record. But nothing was signed yet. Nothing was official. What better bargaining chip? Mike's testimony for lenient treatment of Josh. Maybe the police will pop him with leaving the scene of the accident, but skip the assault charge. In return, Mike testifies in full.

Everyone likes this idea. It's shortly after 2 a.m. and I open up three more bottles of Upper Canada Maple Brown to celebrate. Mike's going to call Lang first thing in the morning.

$ $ $

I get the call from Mike about 11 a.m. I'm still in bed and sluggish after all the drinking and smoking and excitement of last night. I barely hear him as he tells me.

"I just left Lang. Everything's going to be okay. He's going to take care of the jam. Josh is going to be okay."

I let out a huge sigh. Josh is a good guy, he's turned the corner. Sure he slipped up once, but you have to remember the big picture: He's getting his life in order.

I hang up and go back to bed. I sleep very well.

BUYING IN BULK:
WORKING THE PROFIT MARGINS
OF THE DRUG TRADE

By the time Curtis arrived, the others were well into their second pitcher of beer.

It was 7:30 on an April Wednesday night and Tina's was slow, a couple of middle-aged men at the bar and a table of students near the back were the pub's only patrons other than Dave and Jim. Those two had taken a table near the window, the better to watch the women as they strolled past.

"Hello, hello," Curtis said as he sat down. "How are we tonight gentlemen?"

A thin layer of grime coated Curtis's hands and muscular forearms. He'd spent the day working and hadn't had time to stop home for a shower. Dave and Jim noticed the rank smell of sweat immediately, but said nothing.

"Just talking about Scott," said Jim. "Wondering."

Curtis nodded and craned his head, scanning the pub. Tina was behind the bar, reading her Mandarin textbook, still dreaming of leaving the bar behind and working in China. Eventually, she raised her head and spotted Curtis. Waving hello, she emerged from the heavily polished bar with an empty pint glass so he could join in the pitcher.

"Thank you very much ma'am. Could I get a menu?"

"Absolutely," smiled Tina.

A warm breeze blew through the open windows of the bar and turned all heads to the street, where the last of the day's light was being chased by darkness. A quartet of women in tight skirts and high heels were gliding down the sidewalk, surveying the evening's possibilities. The rows of empty seats in Tina's kept them moving along.

"So," said Curtis, after gulping down half a pint. "Do we tell his mom and dad?"

At that, Jim coughed beer between teeth. Curtis never was one for subtlety.

"And what?" said Jim, using a napkin to wipe the brown liquid from his chin. "Tell them what? Their son is missing? We don't know where he is? We think he's *dead*?"

Dave laughed too, joining in.

"Maybe we can say, 'Hello Ms. Brodie. This is Dave, Curtis, and Jim. We're friends of your son. We're quite concerned about his health. You see, he's our drug dealer and we think he might be in serious trouble because he hasn't been returning our calls.'"

"Okay, okay," Curtis said, raising his hands in defeat. "It was only a suggestion. They might know where he is. It might solve the whole problem. I don't know."

"It might make them worry for nothing, too," pointed out Jim. "We really don't know what happened. We only know for sure what Dave has told us."

Both Jim and Curtis took this opportunity to shoot Dave a withering look.

"All right! Enough! I feel bad enough already," Dave said, turning towards the window so he didn't have to meet their eyes.

Scott had gone missing five days ago. It'd been Dave who'd seen him last, as the two left the Underground late Friday night. Scott had been out-of-his-head drunk and high, which in itself was nothing unusual. He regularly consumed his own product and that night he'd been smoking pot, drinking beer and had popped a tab of X for good measure. As they left the bar, Scott wandered off about ten yards and then turned around to address Dave.

Tonight I'm going to die. What are we doing tomorrow?

That was the last thing he'd said. Then Scott had disappeared into the street, lost among the crowds and the cars and the lights.

The incident hadn't struck Dave as that odd at the time. Then again, Dave was in no state to judge. He'd drunk his fair share of gin-and-tonic and was in the process of finishing off a joint when Scott made his mysterious departure. In fact, it didn't cross Dave's mind until the next afternoon, after he'd woken up and started cataloguing the previous night's events. Scott's words did seem a bit odd in the sober light of mid-afternoon, but only the kind of odd that makes for a great story.

You should've seen Scott last night. He was rocked, Dave imagined himself telling people. *He was so out of it he told me he was going to die! And then he asked me what we were doing the next day!* Dave envisioned them all raising their glasses, Scott included, after he told that story with his patented flourish.

If it had been someone else, maybe Dave would have reacted differently. Somebody like Sean or Liam, somebody for whom getting wrecked wasn't a daily occurrence. People like that needed to have their hands held if their trip started to go bad. Not Scott. Scott acting odd was just Scott being Scott. He was the epitome of unusual. An eccentric commerce student who was taking ten years to finish a four-year degree, Scott's bizarre utterances and disturbing takes on life were a regular feature of any night out. At first glance, Friday night at the Underground was par for the course.

Dave went out with a girlfriend Saturday night so he didn't see Scott or Curtis or Jim. The next time he thought about Scott was Sunday night as he crouched over his desk to roll a joint. He'd rented *Fear and Loathing in Las Vegas*, and wanted to be in the right state of mind to watch the film version of Hunter S. Thompson's classic. As he was rolling, Dave noticed he was running a little low on pot. He had maybe a gram-and-a-half left in his Tupperware container. That would not do. He made a mental note to call Scott the next morning.

When he woke up Monday morning, his federal GST rebate cheque had arrived. This was a sign: It was as if the government *intended* Dave to buy drugs this day. So he called Scott, working out how much ecstasy and marijuana he was going to buy in his head while he dialed the number. There was no answer. Dave then paged Scott, and sat back and waited. Thirty minutes passed and no call back. This was a little strange. Dave and Scott got along quite well and Scott usually called him back quickly. Perhaps Scott had turned off his pager while he was in class or working on a presentation. It could be anything.

It was Curtis who became worried first. Of all of them, he was the closest to Scott. They had known each other for years, having both grown up in

The Legalities

NARCOTIC CONTROL ACT, TRAFFICKING

(1) No person shall traffic in a narcotic or any substance represented or held out by the person to be a narcotic.

(2) No person shall have in his possession any narcotic for the purpose of trafficking.

(3) Every person who contravenes subsection (1) or (2) is guilty of an indictable offence and liable to imprisonment for life.

Montreal and bounced around the scene together. Dave and Jim had come to town to go to McGill and had only been hanging around with Scott for a year or two, only after they'd started scoring pharmaceuticals off him.

Curtis and Scott had planned to drive down to Vermont on Sunday, do some shopping in Burlington, and hang out by the lake drinking cold American Budweisers. Curtis needed to get out of Montreal and relax; working construction for the sixth straight summer was starting to get him down. He'd studied English literature at McGill and had hoped to go on to teacher's college, but every year the application deadline came and went with Curtis coming up with some reason to miss it. He always started to regret it when the last of the snow melted away and it hit home that he was spending another summer pounding nails.

It was Scott who had come up with the idea for a trip to clear their heads. The lifestyle got to him once in a while and this was one of those times. He was feeling pretty depressed too and looking for a change of head space. All the drugs, the stress, the paranoia—it was taking its toll. He talked often about getting out of the business and finishing his degree. Curtis knew Scott's family was giving him problems. After all these years, they had to suspect their son was involved in the drug trade, and Scott wasn't handling the situation well. He wanted nothing more than to drive through Vermont, stare up at the sky and mountains, and let his problems slip away.

Curtis woke up about 10 a.m. Sunday morning and put in a call to Scott to confirm their 11 a.m. departure. No answer. Maybe he's still asleep, thought Curtis, as he readied himself to leave. When there was still no answer at 11 a.m., Curtis started paging him. Scott wasn't returning calls. A little angry, Curtis left his apartment. He didn't like being sloughed off by anybody, anytime, but today was worse: he was desperately looking forward to the escape.

Curtis ended up hopping on the Metro and catching an Expos game, but he was still mad when he made it back to his apartment that night. He'd expected a contrite message from Scott. Instead, there was only a message from Dave inviting him over to watch *Fear and Loathing*.

By Monday night, there was still no sign of Scott, and Curtis was genuinely alarmed. He started calling the usual suspects. Jim was the third call he made. No luck there. Curtis called Dave next.

"Well, he was acting a bit odd on Friday night," Dave told Curtis on the phone.

"You know Scott—he was out of his head, rocked. It was a good night."

Dave was about to launch into his well-prepared story, but Curtis cut him off and his tone told Dave it was serious.

"How 'odd?'"

Dave quickly related the story about Scott wandering off.

"What was that? What was the last thing he said to you?"

"He said, 'Tonight I'm going to die. What are we doing tomorrow?' Then he just kind of staggered off, disappeared," explained Dave.

"And you just *let* him? You just let him walk off?"

"Well, I didn't know. I didn't know what to do. He looked all right, I mean, I thought it would be okay. It's Scott. He's always a bit weird."

Curtis was silent. He was tempted to lay into Dave.

"C'mon, it's only been three days. That's not so unusual. He's probably in Toronto or down in the States," Dave said optimistically. "Scott isn't predictable."

Curtis had to concede that. It wasn't like Scott hadn't taken off before. He was known to hop on a train and head off for a Phish concert or take a run down to Baltimore so he could sit in on the filming of his favourite television show, *Homicide: Life on the Streets.* He'd been gone for weeks at a time before. It was also nearing the end of the school year, the time when Scott left for one of his exotic adventures.

The thing was, in the past, Curtis had always known if Scott

Narcotics Schedule

[substances banned under Canada's Narcotic Control Act]

1. **Opium Poppy, its preparations, derivatives, alkaloids and salts, including:**

opium
codeine
morphine
thebaine
acetorphine
acetyldihydrocodeine
benzylmorphine
codoxime
desomorphine
diacetylmorphine (heroin)
dihydrocodeine
dihydromorphine
ethylmorphine
etorphine
hydrocodone
hydromorphone
hydromorphinol
methyldesorphine
methyldihydromorphine
metopon
morphine-N-oxide
myrophine
nalorphine
nicocodine
nicomorphine
norcodeine
normorphine
oxycodone
oxymorphone
pholocodine
thebacon

but not including

apomorphine
cyprenorphine

was gone. Scott would get Curtis to watch his apartment and, more important, water his plants while he was gone. Scott was obsessive about his plants;
he'd never go anywhere for more than a couple of days without making sure
they were well taken care of. He had rows of them in his windows and bedroom, and pampered them like his children. His apartment was like an oxy-
gen-rich greenhouse, with passion-flower vines on the wall and sturdy rubber
plants in the corners, asparagus ferns flowing down from hanging pots and
Christmas cacti erupting off his dining room table. Scott trusted few people
with his plants, and Curtis was one of them.

If Scott had given the plants a good soaking Saturday morning and
then had taken off, they'd still be fine. But the ones in the west window
needed watering twice a week. Another couple of days and they'd start to
suffer. If Scott hadn't gotten in touch with Curtis by then, that would be
serious.

"We'll leave it for now, I guess," Curtis told Dave. "Make sure you call me
if you hear from him."

He hung up and prepared a lunch of ham sandwiches and fruit for work
the next day. It wasn't a crisis yet. Scott could be holed up in his apartment
with some girl, not answering his phone and letting the days wash by in glo-
rious waves of narcotics and sex.

If he didn't hear from him by Wednesday, Curtis would take action. At
least for the plants' sake.

"Have you decided yet?"

Tina was over the table again, smiling again.

Curtis scoured the menu. He'd been working all day, framing at a new
housing development in Longueuil. It was hungry work.

"Do you two want anything?" Curtis asked.

"I'm fine," said Dave, pouring more beer.

"Calamari?" Jim suggested. "Or maybe some zucchini?"

They ordered the fried calamari and a burger for Curtis, plus another
pitcher. The beer arrived quickly and all pints were topped up. Outside, the
street was coming alive and the tables at Tina's were slowly filling up.

"Do you have the key?" It was Jim speaking. Curtis patted his front pocket and felt the outline of the key.

"Don't you worry, I have it."

Curtis had a spare key to Scott's place. It was a deep trust, but one that
reflected both Curtis and Scott's relationship and Scott's fanatical obsession
about his houseplants.

It was Jim's opinion from the beginning that if Curtis was so worried, he should just go over to Scott's apartment to see what was up. It would probably put everybody at ease.

Curtis wasn't sure. He'd been entrusted with the key and had never gone to the apartment without Scott's express consent. He wasn't sure he wanted to violate that trust too early. After all, on any given day there could be five or six thousand dollars' worth of narcotics stashed in the apartment. Curtis didn't want to be accused of snooping.

But it was now Wednesday night and Scott hadn't returned a combined 17 calls and 26 pages from the three of them. After Curtis ate his dinner, they were going to go to Scott's.

"I've never been inside his place," said Dave.

"It's pretty cool. It's like a rainforest inside," said Curtis.

"What if he's there?" wondered Jim.

"Then he'll be touched to know he has such caring, wonderful friends," shrugged Curtis.

"If he's there, maybe we can smoke," said Dave hopefully. He'd run out of his stash yesterday night and was dying to get high.

The food arrived and Curtis got down to the business of swallowing his burger while Jim and Dave picked at the calamari and told each other stories about Scott.

He was a good guy, turning 27 this year, but with his long black hair

naloxone
narcotine
papaverine
poppy seed

2. Coca, its preparations, derivatives, alkaloids and salts, including
coca leave
cocaine
ecgonine

3. Cannabis sativa, its preparations, derivatives, and similar synthetic preparations, including
cannabis resin
cannabis (marijuana)
cannabidiol
cannabinol, nabilone
pyrahexyl
tetrahydrocannabinol

but not including
non-viable Cannabis seed

4. Phenylpiperidines, their preparations, intermediates, derivatives, and salts, including
allyprodine
alphameprodine
alphaprodine
anileridine
betameprodine
betaprodine
benzethidine
diphenoxylate
etoxeridine
furethidine
hydroxypethidine
ketobemidone
methylphenylisonipecotonitrile
morpheridine
norpethidine
pethidine
phenoperidine

and baby face, he regularly passed for 21 or 22. He certainly stood out in his business classes at McGill. All the others were dressing to impress, eager young conservatives ready to conquer the world and fatten their bank accounts. Scott strolled in to class every year with Birkenstocks, jeans and an attitude. He despised most of the other business students and let them know it.

To maintain his standing in the program, he took a class or two each year, but the cut-throat nature of commerce made him ill. These kids thought that with the right investment bankers and a flat tax, all the world's problems would be solved. They were each planning their high-flying business careers upon graduation. Most of them were so straight, they didn't suspect that Scott had a pretty good business of his own on the go.

When he arrived at McGill in 1991, one of his first professors had told the sprawling class of 200 first-year students that the key to success in business was to do something you had a passion for. There were countless ways to make money, he said. Pick one that's right for you. Scott had already started a little business at that point and he had to agree with the professor: Doing something you loved made all the difference.

Scott had loved to smoke dope in high school and had had a great source in his older brother's best friend, Rod. He was always the one who would hook everybody up for parties or dances. If you wanted a little bit of pot or hash for the weekend, call Scott and he would have it for you by the end of the week. He could even get mushrooms or acid on the rare occasion when somebody asked for them.

When he was in high school, he never really saw it as a business. He never made any money off the enterprise; he just happened to get his own drugs for free in return for the volume of sales he brought to Rod.

University was a disappointment at first. Scott's dad worked as a butcher at the Provigo and his mom did telemarketing at night. It meant the family didn't have the money to send Scott away to Halifax for school like he wanted. He ended up picking McGill over Concordia because of its classic campus and used the money he made painting houses to pay for his first-year tuition.

When the first day of school arrived, he was somewhat depressed. Instead of a new city and a new life, it was the same old Montreal. What he didn't realize as he started into the Frosh Week activities was that with thousands of out-of-town kids away from home and eager to party, there was going to be a niche to fill. These kids loved to smoke and have fun, but they didn't know the first thing about scoring drugs in Montreal.

Meanwhile, Scott was involved in all the festivities and always had an ample supply of dope. At a couple of frosh parties, he smoked a group of his new friends up and from there word spread that he carried. By the end of that first week, more than 40 people had approached Scott asking to buy.

It was a little flattering for Scott. He'd always liked being the go-to guy at high school. It made him feel needed. Now here he was in an intimidating new situation, wanting to make a good impression. What else could he do? When people asked him, Scott said he'd talk to his source and see if he could score for them. That week, he stopped by to see his brother's buddy Rod.

During high school, he'd never had to get more than nine or ten grams in a week. The deal was always the same. He'd buy it for $12 a gram from Rod and sell it to his friends for $12 a gram. He usually got a little bag of pot thrown his way for the effort, and that was all he wanted. He didn't feel right making money off his friends.

This was a bit different. These were mostly strangers. And if he was to satisfy everybody who'd approached him, he'd need at least 50 grams of marijuana, probably more. He certainly didn't want to put up the $600 it would cost to buy the drugs. To be honest, he didn't even know if he could get that much from Rod.

When Scott sat down in Rod's

    piminodine
    properidine
    trimeperidine
    carbamethidine
oxpheneridine

5. **Phenazepines, its preparations, derivatives, and salts, including**
    proheptazine
    ethoheptazine
    metethoheptazine
    metheptazine

6. **Amidones, their preparations, intermediates, derivatives and salts, including**
    dimethylaminodiphenylbutanonitrile
    dipipanone
    isomethadone
    methadone
    normethadone
    phenadoxone

7. **Methadols, their preparations, derivatives, and salts, including**
    acetylmethadol
    alphacetylmethadol
    alphamethadol
    betacetylmethadol
    betamethadol
    dimepheptanol
    noracymethadol

8. **Phenalkoxams, their preparations, derivatives and salts, including**
    dimenoxadol
    dioxaphetylebutyrate
    dextropropoxyphene

9. **Thiambutenes, their preparations, derivatives, and salts, including**
    diethylthiambutene
    dimethylthiambutene
    ethylmethylthiambutene

basement apartment and laid out what people wanted, Rod let rip with a huge smile.

"It looks like you can make some money off this," he said.

Scott stared blankly. "What?"

Rod went on to explain the "volume sales" principle.

"Think of a case of Pepsi, right. It costs, what, $6.99, seven dollars in the store? But what about when you buy it from a machine? A buck a can, right? So that same 24 cans can be worth $24, if you sell it the right way.

"Same thing with dope. I sell you a gram for what, $12? Maybe $14 if it's really dry? Shit, the thing is, I can get an ounce for $180, $200."

Rod ran through the math quickly. An ounce was 28 grams. If you broke up the ounce into 28 single-gram portions, you could sell it for $336 at $12 a gram. That was a profit of $156 on an ounce. If you charged $13 a gram, the profit went up to $184 for the ounce. If you could push the price to $14 or $15 a gram . . .

"I get the picture," said Scott, amazed at how much money Rod had made from selling him drugs over the past couple of years.

"Look, I give it to you at $12 because you Darwin's little brother, man. I sell to most people for $14 a gram. People will pay. It's good dope, so I don't do any favours. I don't think you should be doing any favours either. You got these rich kids wanting dope, you should be getting something from it."

"I don't know. I don't feel real good about that."

"Never do anything for free, my man. What you're doing is work. What you're doing is dangerous. You've *got* to be compensated."

Scott thought about it a bit more. Everybody who talked to him wanted to buy at least two grams. Say he *could* sell a hundred grams. He could buy four ounces for less than $800. But he could turn around and sell a hundred of those grams for $1,200 or $1,300 and still have 12 grams of pot left over for his own personal use.

"So, you'd sell me an ounce for $180?" Scott asked Rod, warming to the idea.

Rod laughed. "I don't like you that much Scottie. Think more like $220."

"What? I though you just said—"

"—that you should never do anything for free. Exactly."

Scott understood.

The next day at school, he made a point of bumping into most of the people who wanted to score off him. Was $13 okay? The answer was always yes. By the end of the day he had more than 120 grams in orders.

He went to the Royal Bank that afternoon to make the withdrawal. He was nervous and scared. The plan was to buy five ounces, 140 grams, for $1,100. That was a lot of money, more than he'd ever held in his hand at one time before.

Working as a student painter all summer had left Scott with about $3,500 in the bank to pay for school that year. This deal would seriously eat away at that balance if it didn't go right. As the teller counted out the fifties and twenties he pictured himself being arrested by the police. What would his parents say? From the bank, he walked to one of the head shops to buy a scale. For only $30, you could get a nifty pocket scale that handled measurements of up to two ounces. He would need it when he broke up the marijuana to sell at school.

By the time he got to Rod's place, it was getting dark and the money felt like a ten-pound weight in his front pocket.

Rod was in the basement watching *Star Trek*. He waved Scott in and went to the freezer. He appeared with a zip-lock bag with more dope inside than Scott had seen in his entire life.

"I got it measured out. It's a good weight, don't worry. You have the money?"

Scott pulled out his $1,100, his eyes never leaving the bag of marijuana. It was enormous. Half of him just wanted to run away to the woods and smoke the month away.

10. Moramides, their preparations, intermediates, derivatives and salts, including
   dextromoramide
   diphenylmorpholinoisovaleric acid
   levomoramide
   racemoramide

11. Morphinians, their preparations, derivatives and salts, including
   levomethorphan
   levorphanal
   levophenacylmorphan
   norlevorphanol
   phenomorphan
   racemethorphan
   racemorphan

but not including
   dextromethorphan
   dextrorphan
   levallorphan
   levargorphan
   butorphanol
   nalbuphine

12. Benzazocines, their preparations, derivatives and salts, including
   phenazocine
   metazocine
   pentazocine

but not including
   cyclazocine

13. Ampromides, their preparations, derivatives and salts, including
   diampromide
   phenampromide
   propiram

14. Benzimidazoles, their preparations, derivatives and salts, including
   clonitazene
   etonitazene

"I triple wrapped it to cut down on the smell, but it's pretty fresh. I wouldn't go riding the bus with it."

Scott nodded and shoved the dope into his knapsack. His hand was sweaty when he shook Rod's.

"Relax, Scottie. You have nothing to worry about."

That night in his room, he opened the windows and lit incense to cover the smell of the fresh marijuana. Then, he lit a joint and took out his bounty. Unbelievable. It took him two hours to measure it out into single-gram portions. As he looked at the stack of zip-lock bags on his bed, he felt a little bit dirty. At least it was only marijuana, he told himself. He stashed the marijuana under his bed, but he couldn't sleep that night he was so nervous. And excited. If he earned good money at this, it would mean he could finally move out of his parents' home.

It took him 10 days to go through that first batch of 140 grams. He saw some people on campus, told them he'd hooked up and word spread quickly. He took in more than $1,700, a profit of $600 in less than two weeks. He called up Rod and bought another five ounces with those profits. This time it was gone in a week. Another $600 in his pocket. Scott couldn't believe it. Most people left university owing $25,000 in student loans. Scott figured he could leave with $25,000 in the bank.

It was all good those first couple of months, until one day he was in the line at one of the campus coffee stands. This guy came up to him, all nervous-like, and started mumbling.

"What? What?" asked Scott.

"Uh, man, like, can I score off you?"

"What are you talking about?"

The kid looked sick. "I just thought, you know, you like, sort of sold . . ."

Scott just stared at him.

" . . . sold, well. I wanted to buy some dope."

Scott was carrying about 20 grams in his knapsack but this was wrong. "I don't know what you're talking about."

"Oh." The kid looked down at his feet and walked away.

It was the first time paranoia set it. How many people knew? There was only one answer to that question: Too many.

From then on, it was a low profile. He'd started selling regularly to about 15, 20 guys in residence. That was all right, he thought. But he wasn't going to sell to anybody he didn't know. He didn't want trouble.

It turned out to be a better system. His regular customers became known as the guys who could score and Scott faded into the background. He started to give it to his regulars for $12 a gram and they marked it up if they wanted, sometimes as high as $15 a gram. By the end of Scott's first year at McGill, the volume got to be too much, even for Rod. Although he was making $200 or $300 a week just selling the ounces to Scott, Rod was getting tired of the business. Scott was relentless. He had such a steady stable of eager university students

15. Phencyclidine, its salts and derivatives

16. Fentanyl

17. Sufentanil

18. Tilidine

19. Carfentanil

20. Alfentanil

that he seemed continually in need of marijuana. So Rod talked to his dealer and asked if he could handle Scott directly.

Scott didn't mind. All it did was cut out the middleman and that was one of the first lessons he'd learned at McGill: Always cut out the middleman. His ounces dropped by about $40 each, but Scott used another lesson he learned at McGill. Instead of pocketing the new profits, he reinvested. He cut another dollar off the price he sold to his regulars, a little bonus for handling so much business and keeping Scott out of the spotlight.

By the end of his first year, he'd moved to a great apartment downtown, just blocks from McGill. His business was great, mostly marijuana with a small core of kids who bought mushrooms and hash. After final exams, Scott had more than $11,000 in his bank account. He bought a ticket to Europe and spent the summer backpacking, with a considerable amount of time devoted to Amsterdam.

That had pretty much been his life since 1991. A course or two at McGill, a new crop of students arriving at campus every year, eager for pharmaceuticals—a leisurely life of pleasure. There was a bit of a twist in 1995 when a new drug came to town: Ecstasy. It was huge on the rave scene and kids were reading about it in *Spin* and *Rolling Stone*. It was supposed to be a smooth ride that kept you happily buzzed and energized for a couple of hours. Scott also heard it enhanced the senses. Everything you touched felt better and sex was rumoured to be absolutely sublime.

X sold for between $30 and $40 a pill on campus, but there was never enough to go around. Scott saw an opportunity for expansion. He could buy a hundred tabs of X for $2,000 from his dealer. If he sold them at $30, that'd be an easy thousand in his pocket.

Within weeks, his ecstasy sales were rivaling his marijuana sales. Business was simply incredible. On average, he was selling about 100 grams of marijuana and 50 tabs of X a week during the school year. It meant close to $3,000 a week in cash was moving through his hands and his profit margin was good: He was clearing about $1,000 a week.

He did fill special requests. There were always some people who wanted to try out cocaine or mescaline, and Scott always thought it would be better if they got it from a safe source, so he hooked them up. He knew it was a more dangerous drug, but he felt a bit virtuous. He'd heard stories of people lacing cocaine with all kinds of shit. One dealer he knew put in tiny amounts of powdered glass—he'd rub two clear glass ashtrays over the coke—so it would make people's noses bleed. "They always think it's really good shit if they bleed," the guy had told Scott.

There was no doubt cocaine was another moneymaker, but it made Scott a little nervous. He could buy an ounce for $1,100 and break it down into 28 grams and sell it for $80 a pop. That was doubling your money, and kids on coke always came back for more. Thing was, that was a little bit risky. He'd known people who'd gotten rolled because of cocaine, and his market didn't have the money. If they did want to buy, it was half-grams for $40 or the occasional girl wanting to buy a quarter for $20. It wasn't worth the trouble.

Scott lived in a swanky, plant-filled apartment in a converted Victorian house downtown. The rent was only $750 a month for a five-and-a-half, and he had a great balcony. Scott didn't drive a car and his wardrobe consisted of Gap khakis, jeans, sandals, and a colourful array of T-shirts. In the winter, he had a couple of worn wool sweaters and a toque. *GQ* would never be calling him. His only other expense was his tuition and that cost him less than $1,000 a year.

It all made for a pretty good income and a pretty good lifestyle. School and business during the fall, winter and spring and then an exotic vacation every summer with his profits: Indonesia, China, South Africa, Argentina, Mexico, Portugal—he spent every summer exploring.

When he got into the business it was just to pay for school and an apartment. It turned out to be such a good life he didn't want to let it go. He dropped from a full-time student to a part-time student after first year. Three years later, he dropped from part-time to a single course a year. At this rate, he was on pace to graduate in 2004.

But now it was 1999. And he was missing.

The burger done, the beer drunk and only a few crumbs of calamari left, Curtis, Dave and Jim called for the bill. Scott lived four blocks away.

They waved goodbye to Tina and broke into the stream of people on the street, letting the crowd carry them north towards Scott's. He lived on the third floor of the three-storey building. The first floor housed a vegetarian restaurant. There were students living in the apartments on the second floor and Scott and a bicycle courier/aspiring artist on the third. There was a gleam of light in the bicycle courier's apartment but Scott's windows were dark.

They went in through the main door, which was open as usual. Scott and the other tenants were always pleading with the landlord to get the door fixed. Many mornings they found a drunken wino or college student passed out in the building's tiny foyer. The landlord managed to keep putting it off.

Up the stairs to Scott's. They knocked loudly. No answer. Curtis knocked again, just to be safe, but that only brought the bike courier to his door. He was dressed in boxers and an old Terence Trent Darby concert T-shirt. His toenails were painted a shocking lime green.

"Greg, right?" asked Curtis.

The bike courier nodded.

"You haven't seen Scott have you?"

The bike courier scratched himself and shook his head.

"Oh. Okay."

The bike courier stayed in his doorway.

Curtis raised his hand to show off the spare key. "I'm just going to let myself in to check up on him. He gave me a key."

The bike courier shrugged and retreated into his apartment.

Curtis unlocked the door and swung it open.

There was an unpleasant odour, sickly sweet, like milk long gone bad.

"Scott?"

Curtis stepped in while Dave and Jim waited in the hall. Curtis searched out the light switch in the darkness. He popped it on.

"Shit."

Scott was on the couch, fully dressed in jeans and a sweater. He was curled up in a fetal position. His face was pale and bloated. He looked dead.

Curtis stepped over the coffee table and tried to shake him. Scott didn't move, and his flesh was cold. He *was* dead.

"You'd better come in," Curtis said.

Dave and Jim stared at the body.

"Oh my God. Oh shit. This isn't good." Dave stood there, mouth gaping. "I've never seen a dead body before."

"Shut up, Dave," Jim said quietly.

Curtis got up and shut the door.

The coffee table was littered with paraphernalia. A small jar of pot, another jar filled with ecstasy, some speed in tin foil. What looked like cocaine, cut into lines, on the table.

"Should we clean this up?"

"What about the police?"

Curtis sat down on the couch beside Scott and buried his face in his hands. "I think maybe we should call his parents now."

Jim and Dave stood awkwardly by the door. "Do you want us . . .?"

Curtis looked up. "No, you don't even know them. Why don't you go home. I'll take care of this."

Dave reached for the door handle.

"Are you sure?" asked Jim.

"Yeah. It's better this way."

Jim and Dave left.

Curtis searched for the phone book to get the number of Scott's parents. He'd only spoken to them a couple of times before. He'd met them at Scott's place once and had been out to dinner with them for Scott's 25th birthday.

It was past 11. He hoped they weren't sleeping.

After six rings, a man's voice answered.

"Mr. Brodie? . . . This is Curtis, Curtis Addison. I'm a friend of Scott's . . . No, I know he's not there . . . There's a problem . . . No, not the police again. I think you should come over to Scott's. I think he's dead."

There was a long silence on the other end.

Mr. Brodie finally spoke. Curtis nodded and then hung up. They wouldn't be coming. Last year, Scott's parents had found a half-kilo of marijuana he'd stashed in their basement freezer. It was the fourth time they'd caught him with drugs. His mother had given him an ultimatum: Give up the drugs and go to rehab or forget your family. Scott didn't go to rehab. His parents hadn't seen him since.

Curtis picked up the phone again and called 911. No, he told the operator, this was not an emergency.

As he waited for police to arrive, Curtis went into the kitchen and picked up the watering can. Scott's plants were starting to dry out.

ART FOR MONEY'S SAKE: LIFE AFTER A MILLION-DOLLAR TAX FRAUD

It's not often you get to see a box with more than a million dollars inside, but if Norman is to be believed, that's exactly what he's holding in his arms.

He's standing in a drab, ten-by-ten office that he rents in an industrial park on the outskirts of Montreal. The grey sports jacket he's wearing is slightly rumpled and his green-and-gold tie hangs askew. He wears his greying hair short at the ears and back, but keeps his mustache long, giving his pudgy, 44-year-old face a stern look it would otherwise be lacking. There's a cigarette hanging out of his mouth, but this is nothing new. Norman has been chain-smoking all day. He has already exhausted the contents of one pack of Rothmans Specials and is now well into his second.

The office itself is not much bigger than the bathroom at your average roadside gas station and with a desk, a chair, and a filing cabinet all crammed inside, the room is unbearably cramped. These are the headquarters of Norman's now-defunct international art exportation business. He's back here today to show off that very art.

After entering the office and flipping on the fluorescent overhead light, Norman has to squeeze awkwardly by his guest to reach a brown cardboard box about the size of a microwave tucked underneath the desk. The flaps of the box are open and a stack of thick, creamy white paper is visible. He pulls out the box triumphantly and places it on the desk.

"Here they are," he says with a broad smile. "I knew I had some left."

Norman slips the first piece of paper from the stack and turns it over. It's a lithograph of a rural landscape, complete with a log cottage, a team of horses at work in a distant field and a rock-strewn stream burbling in the foreground. If you examine the lines of the ink sketch carefully, you can see the artist has hidden pictures of naked, large-breasted women at various points in the drawing. There's one in the curves of the stream and another in the cross-hatching near the top of the cottage's roof.

Norman holds the picture at arm's length and lets out a soft, humming sigh. "Beautiful work, no?" asks Norman.

Actually, no. To the casual observer, the work is raw and uninspired, the sort of rough doodling that someone might accomplish while watching reruns on television or taking part in a dull long-distance conversation. Norman seems disappointed.

"They are *good*. The artist is very good, from the Eastern Townships. We discovered him ourselves," he says. "Today, everybody thinks they are an expert." He huffs his displeasure and examines the lithograph again. "To each his own. Me, I think Picasso is ugly," Norman says. "Something like this looks beautiful in any room."

He drops the lithograph back into the box, then drops the box onto the floor. He shoves it back under the desk with the side of his well-worn black Oxford shoe. There are more than 1,000 such pictures in the box and according to Norman, each one is worth precisely $1,197.12. That would mean the cardboard box contains at least $1.19-million worth of art.

Norman maneuvers himself back past the desk and flicks off the office light. He stands at the door and waits impatiently. Down the hallway, you can see doorways to other tiny offices. There are dozens in this complex, each identical, and each equipped with little more than a phone and a desk. Norman pays less than $300 in rent each month for the space.

"All right, that's enough," he says as he locks the door. "I don't care what anyone else says. They're very valuable."

Norman knows the routine is wearing a bit thin. He is a gentle man, with a wife and a pleasant home just a few kilometres from this very office. He scratches his mustache and exhales.

"Okay, okay, even if I am guilty of everything they say, who did I hurt? I dare you to find one supplier or one small business who lost a nickel. Even when we were charged by Revenue Canada, no one else got dragged in. Who was hurt?" He pauses, thinking about what he has just said. "That's not saying I did anything wrong of course. It's just hypothetical, you understand, but it's something to think about."

Norman pulls out another cigarette and lights it off the dying embers of the one already in his mouth. He squints as the smoke curls into his eye.

"I have to go. I've been away from my wife too long. I don't want her to worry."

With that he walks off, heading towards the exit stairwell of the building. As he's halfway to the door, he turns and addresses his guest again.

"I did nothing wrong. I want people to know that."

After all this time, Norman is still in denial.

It's been three months since he pleaded guilty to several fraud charges in connection with one of the biggest GST scams in Canadian history. Norman masterminded a scheme where he claimed to be exporting valuable Canadian art to the United States and then applied for government tax refunds based on overinflated estimates of the art's value. In total, he submitted claims for more than $5.3 million in GST refunds over a four-year period. He received approximately $2.2 million of that money before tax officials became suspicious.

Despite standing up in court and pleading guilty, despite having his lawyer negotiate a sweetheart of a deal where he received only probation for his crimes, and despite an exhaustive Revenue Canada investigation that tracked down every lie in his labyrinth of deceptions, Norman still maintains he did nothing wrong. And he does it with such a straight face it's almost charming.

"It was a misunderstanding. A big, big, misunderstanding," Norman repeats over and over again. "Revenue Canada just didn't understand what we were doing. It was a business and we were businessmen."

The Legalities: Fraud

CANADIAN CRIMINAL CODE, SECTION 380

(1) Every one who, by deceit, falsehood or other fraudulent means, whether or not it is a false pretence within the means of this Act, defrauds the public or any person, whether ascertained or not, of any property, money or valuable security.

(a) is guilty of an indictable offence and liable to a term of imprisonment not exceeding ten years... (where the) value of the subject-matter of the offence exceeds five thousand dollars or

(b) is guilty

(i) of an indictable offence and liable to imprisonment for a term not exceeding two years, or of an offence punishable on summary conviction where the value of the subject-matter of the offence does not exceed five thousand dollars.

$ $ $

Norman grew up on a farm in Eastern Ontario in the '50s and '60s. Watching his father and mother work the land and take care of the livestock taught him everything he needed to know about operating a successful business. Devotion, persistence, stubbornness—that was what Norman knew worked in the real world. Alone on that remote farm, it was his family against the land and his family won the battle.

As a child, then teenager, Norman was always fascinated by the financial operations of the farm. He took a keen interest in how fluctuating market prices for corn and milk affected his family's bottom line. It wasn't surprising that after completing high school in the early '70s, he chose to go to Toronto to study business. He yearned to strike out and earn his fortune. From early on, his father had inspired in him a great love for the independence of business. It was the individual against the world, and Norman wanted to test his mind and sweat against the minds and sweat of others.

After finishing a college business program, he started out in sales. He began at a major department store, first selling suits and trousers in the men's section, then getting promoted to the office where he worked in the credit department. His days were spent cajoling people into applying for the store's credit card at a mere 29 per cent annual rate of interest. For Norman, it was all about the art of the sale. He loved to use guile and charm to convince customers to trust him with their money.

"What I learned early on in this business is that it's all about sales. I can sell swimming pools to Eskimos," Norman boasts.

With his self-professed gift for sales, he quickly became bored working at the department store. Sure, he was earning a good income off his commissions, but he knew if he wanted to make real money and have real freedom, he would have to strike out on his own.

Because he had more contacts in Quebec than Ontario, he decided to move from Toronto to Montreal in the late '70s. There he took another job in the credit business, this time as a financing executive helping young couples with credit problems acquire loans for that new car or home. His plan was to spend his days earning his paycheque and his nights and weekends earning his fortune.

With the support of his wife and his brothers, Norman began setting up a series of small businesses—everything from dry cleaning outlets to a plant that manufactured three-ring binders for school children. The businesses grew slowly, but after a couple of years, he was confident enough to give up the safety of his paycheque and venture out completely on his own. In 1982, he became a self-employed entrepreneur. He also became a target of Revenue Canada for the first time.

After quitting his job to focus full-time on his companies, he put in a claim for an $80,000 tax refund based on his business expenses and income. With all the start-up costs of the new businesses and the fact that he no longer had a steady income, Norman believed he was eligible to get back most everything he'd invested to that point.

Revenue Canada disagreed and decided to audit. After four years and countless meetings with lawyers, Norman's $80,000 claim was reduced to $200. He was bitterly frustrated. Growing up on the farm, he'd always heard his father complain about government bureaucracy and regulations. Now Norman could relate.

"There was so much stress. It was the worst four years of my life," Norman says now. "It's a dark cloud having Revenue over your head."

The struggle soured Norman on the government, but not on the miracles of capitalism. He continued to build his businesses with the help of his brothers. They had different projects scattered across Montreal, each one eking out a small profit.

"I went to bed exhausted every night, but happy," he says.

That all went awry in the early 1990s. The country was plummeting into a recession and Norman's business empire took a beating. Customers weren't spending as much and Norman was being killed by the high interest rates he was paying on his business loans. It was at about that time that Prime Minister Brian Mulroney and the Conservative government decided to put a new tax in place—the Goods and Services Tax.

The GST was immediately despised by the general public, who hated having to tack on an additional seven per cent to everything they spent. The

TOTAL ANNUAL GST COLLECTION

1998 - $19.5 billion
1997 - $18.1 billion
1996 - $16. 4 billion
1995 - $16.8 billion
1994 - $15.7 billion
1993 - $14.9 billion
1992 - $15.2 billion
1991 - $2.6 billion

(Source: Public Accounts of Canada, 1997–98)

tax was supposed to replace a hidden manufacturing tax, but a skeptical citizenry thought it was plain old government gouging.

The tax was hated even more by the small-business community, who were worried that in the middle of a recession, the tax would only serve to scare away what few consumers there were left. The additional load of paperwork and accounting didn't help either. Each small business was responsible for collecting and keeping track of the seven per cent tax—yet another headache.

For Norman, who at this point had a hand in dozens of small businesses, it was a nightmare. Already battered by the recession, the new tax put more stress on him and his enterprises. He struggled every week to keep the books balanced and it seemed the only time he was at home was to sleep. With his bank accounts drained, his businesses teetering, it wasn't a surprise his marriage began to crumble under the added strain. Soon Norman was headed for divorce as well.

The more time he spent being forced to learn about it, the more he hated the GST. But being a businessman, he decided to put the anger to good use. He wrote a book called *The Secrets of the GST Revealed*, publishing it and marketing it himself. The book explained the new tax, but more important, it listed dozens of ways businesses could save money by exploiting loopholes in the GST legislation. He produced the book in English and French and made a tidy profit from his foray into publishing. After that episode, he considered himself to be something of a GST guru.

The next move was almost inevitable. His other businesses were in trouble, his home life was in ruins, and his decade-long grudge against the federal government and Revenue Canada was burning hotter than ever. Norman decided he needed a change. With his newfound insight into Canadian tax laws, it was time to try something a little more challenging and perhaps a little less ethical. He liked to call it his "art business."

$ $ $

Under the Excise Tax Act, all companies earning more than $30,000 a year must register with Revenue Canada and file either a monthly, quarterly, or annual GST return. While it's the federal government that receives the bounty, it's the restaurants, the bookstores and the used car lots that collect it. A business is forced to charge seven per cent tax on almost every purchase or service rendered. There are precious few exceptions to the tax, only essential items such as bread and milk.

It isn't a straight collection system though. A business is not required to send the government every dollar of GST it receives from its customers or clients. Instead, the tax laws are structured so that a business can deduct any GST they have paid on items needed to operate the business.

For example, a women's shoe store in Vancouver may buy shoes at $60 a pair from a Canadian manufacturer and then sell them at $100 a pair to the customer. If the store has $100,000 in sales in the year—that would be 1,000 pairs of shoes—it would collect $7,000 in GST from its customers. But since the store is charged the tax by the manufacturer when it buys those 1,000 pairs of shoes for $60,000, the shoe store also has to pay out $4,200 in GST. With this scenario, the shoe store would then only have to remit $2,800 in GST to the government—the $7,000 they collected minus the $4,200 they paid.

Canadian tax laws do allow for certain transactions where a business does not have to charge GST at all. Included among these exceptions to the GST rule are cases when a business in Canada sells to people or businesses outside

A Way to Bite a Bit off the Top of Your Taxes

Find an artist in need of money. Find out what painting he or she's selling for $7,500, and offer a quick deal—$1,500 cash. The artist thinks about rent or an upcoming trip, and it doesn't take long before the deal is done. One condition, though: You want your receipt to say $7,500, not $1,500.

You walk out, and a couple of months later you donate that painting to a local gallery or city hall or some other organization with tax-receipt writing powers. They get it appraised and the value comes back $7,500. After all, that's what you paid and that's what the artist says it's worth. You write that off against your taxes at the end of the year and you're up a couple of bucks.

A simple scheme, one so easy to pull off and so hard to police that according to the Canadian Museums Association, in 1995, the federal government considered limiting the tax credit program. Each year, millions of dollars' worth of art is donated to public institutions, but many of the seemingly generous gifts are motivated by little more than catching a couple breaks on a tax return.

Fuelling the scheme is the dismal state of the domestic art market. The combination of desperate artists and a corner-cutting bourgeoisie makes it one of the more conniving ways to rip somebody off.

of the country. That means someone in Tennessee who wants to buy a Toronto Maple Leafs jersey directly from the hockey club by mail order would not have to pay GST on the purchase.

In the same case of the women's shoe store in Vancouver, if the business was in fact an Internet store and sold all of its shoes online to customers in the United States, the store would not have to charge any GST on the $100,000 in sales. In that case, it would not have collected the $7,000 in GST but it still would have had to pay the $4,200 in GST to the manufacturer when it purchased those shoes. Then, the Excise Tax Act allows the shoe store to file for a refund and get that $4,200 back because the purchase of the shoes was central to the operation of the business.

Having authored his book *The Secrets of the GST Revealed*, Norman knew all about this little taxation oddity. And he set out to exploit every inch of it with his art exportation business.

Norman began by producing hundreds of "works of art"—pictures of eagles, dolphins, whales, and an assortment of landscapes from historical rural Quebec. Among these landscapes was the ink sketch of the cottage, the stream, and the naked women hidden in the drawing. He got local artists to draw or sketch the originals and then made thousands of lithograph copies of each one. The copies were made on high-quality paper and numbered, but they were still cheap to produce—less than $20 each even after paying the artist for the original work.

The next step was to set up a series of art companies. Norman and his brother traveled across Canada and the United States, registering business after business under different names. Most of the addresses they used were nothing more than postal drops, the kind of place where you can rent a box for $25 a month and they collect your mail for you. As for the phone numbers used on the business registration forms, the majority of them were just cellular phone numbers. Using $20-a-month phone plans with an answering service—he never had to make any outgoing calls from the businesses—he could receive and check messages for each business from anywhere in Canada. A handful of the businesses did have office space, but nothing larger than the cramped room on the outskirts of Montreal.

All told, Norman and his brother created 186 different shell companies spread out around North America: There were 77 in Toronto, 26 in Ottawa, 16 in Quebec, one in New Brunswick, one in British Columbia, and 65 in the United States.

The companies were used to take full advantage of the tax refund system. They were divided into three groups—A companies, B companies and C companies, and there were roughly 60 companies in each group. If the setup was to be compared to the Vancouver shoe store scenario, the "A" companies were the shoe manufacturer, the "B" companies were the shoe store and the "C" companies were the people in the United States who bought the shoes. Of course, in this scenario, the product was art and the manufacturer, store, and customer were essentially all the same person—Norman.

The "A" companies were located in Canada and acted as the starting point for the lithographs. These were the manufacturing companies, the ones that made the copies of the lithographs and set the price of them at $1,197.12 each.

The "B" companies were also located in Canada and acted as the middlemen. They bought the lithographs from the "A" companies for the set price of $1,197.12 each and then sold them to the "C" companies in the United States for between $1,400 and $2,000 each. The "A" companies gave the "B" companies receipts showing they had paid the $1,197.12 plus GST—it worked out to $83.80—for each lithograph. The "B" companies also had their receipts showing they in turn sold the lithographs to the "C" companies for between $1,400 and $2,000—but without charging GST because the "C" companies were in the United States and were therefore exempt from the tax.

....

Beauty is in the Eye of the Beholder —
Or at Least, a Good Investment Opportunity

Most Canadians know the name Emily Carr, but do they really know her body of work? One Saskatchewan entrepreneur gambled that some people would buy Canadian art, like that of Emily Carr, without doing too much background homework.

From his Regina art dealership, the man commissioned young artists to recreate works by Carr and a handful of other prominent painters. He would then sell those paintings to uninitiated investors for between $200 and $2,400, with assurances that it was the steal of a lifetime. One man paid $2,400 for a half-interest in a painting that was promised to be worth $60,000. It was actually worth less than $20.

In the early 1990s, Joseph Olah, Jr., pleaded guilty to six counts of fraud and was sentenced to eight months in jail.

The "C" companies would allegedly then distribute the lithographs to American customers who apparently couldn't get enough tawdry Canadian art.

The nut of the scam was that no money was ever being exchanged among all these companies. But plenty of fake receipts were. It was with these receipts that Norman made his money. For every lithograph that went from the "A" company to the "B" company to the "C" company, he was eligible for an $83.80 refund because the "B" company had receipts to show it had paid the GST to the "A" company *and* the "B" company had receipts to show it hadn't charged the "C" company GST. Technically, for that same transaction the "A" company owed the government the $83.80 in GST it had supposedly collected from the "B" company. This is where more fake receipts would come in. For that $83.80 the "A" company owed, it would come up with fake business receipts of its own—say, a $1,000 receipt for fictional art supplies that would give them a $70 GST credit that they could deduct from the $83.80 in taxes they owed.

The scam was incredibly profitable. For every 1,000 lithographs the "B" companies supposedly bought from the "A" companies and shipped to the "C" companies, Norman was eligible for $83,800 in GST refunds. Since the "A" companies always managed to balance their GST claims with bogus receipts from artists, printers, art supply stores, appraisers and anyone else that would charge the GST, most of that $83,800 went straight into Norman's pocket.

Over a four-year period, the 186 companies connected to Norman had more than 60,000 of these lithographs pass through their hands and down to the States—meaning they'd claimed more than $5 million in refunds from the federal government. With all of those 186 companies producing a mountain of paperwork, they simply flooded Revenue Canada with documentation that would take thousands of hours to verify.

While money was never exchanged among the "A", "B" and "C" companies, the lithographs were in fact mailed to get genuine shipping and customs receipts. Norman had chosen wisely with art: it was light so cheap to ship, and it was something whose value was open to debate. To an unsuspecting customs clerk who examined the lithographs, they may well think it could be worth almost $1,200. After all, reasoned Norman, it seems anything goes for expensive art these days.

But the truth was, those precious lithographs were actually worth a hell of a lot less than $1,197.12. They were actually worth less than $20. *Well* less than $20.

When Revenue Canada investigators began looking into Norman, they took the lithographs to several leading art appraisers.

"They came back with the figure of $20," says one investigator from Revenue Canada. "And one appraiser told us even that was considered a *very* generous estimate. That art wasn't much more than a pile of high-end photocopies."

That meant Norman's costs were minuscule: producing the cheap lithographs, mailing them among the three levels of companies to get legitimate shipping receipts for the "B" companies, and the cost of registering each of the 186 shell companies and keeping their post office boxes and cellphones operating. Add in the occasional trip to the States or across Canada to set up new shell companies, and that was it.

It was hard, complicated work, sure, but it was rewarding work. It netted Norman more than $2.2 million before it all came crashing down.

$ $ $

Norman is chain-smoking again, but this time at least he has an excuse. He's forgotten his lighter and matches at home, he explains, so he's only lighting the cigarettes off each other so he doesn't have to keep getting up and bothering other people for a light. It's not that he's nervous, honestly.

He's sitting in a Dunkin' Donuts outlet located three-and-a-half blocks from the bungalow he shares with his new wife. It's the day after he's showed off the box full of lithographs that were worth more than $1 million, at least according to his old tax claims.

"Okay, maybe they're not worth quite that, but who knows?" he says with a little bit of a chuckle. "But how do you know what anything costs these days? I have a friend who just bought his son an old Patrick Roy card for $160. Why is that worth $160? It's only paper and ink; who decides these things?"

With a large black coffee in front of him and a tiny aluminum ashtray overflowing with cigarette butts at his elbow, Norman is trying to explain where the $2.2 million went.

They'd always had a reputation for high living. It used to be, if it wasn't a Cadillac, it wasn't good enough. Even at the Dunkin' Donuts, Norman is wearing two fat gold-and-diamond rings on his fingers. After going through Norman's credit card bills, one Revenue Canada investigator on the case quipped, "This was the kind of guy that when he felt like Thai food, he'd fly to Bangkok."

Norman admits he liked the money—"Sure, my brother and I are steak-

and-champagne guys," he says—but he insists that he never got to spend much of their GST windfall.

When they were finally caught, Norman says he had $400,000 in his bank that the government took and another $125,000 in uncashed GST cheques in his office. He also says he invested $500,000 in a paint company and lost every penny. And the other $1,175,000?

"I used that to run the art business," he says.

More than one million to run a phony art scam?

"There were a lot of expenses. A lot of travel to all the different spots. You can look," Norman says. "You won't find anything left. It's all gone."

Norman pleaded guilty to the fraud charges just before Christmas 1997. He says he was given an option: pay a $60,000 fine and be put on 18 months' probation, or be put in jail for 18 months. Norman paid the fine. He says if he'd had a previous criminal record, he wouldn't have been given the option.

His art exportation business came apart after Revenue Canada became suspicious during routine audits starting in the mid-90s. The scheme Norman came up with was a relatively common one on a smaller scale and the department's auditors were under standing orders to look into any company that made regular claims for GST refunds. After auditors noticed some of Norman's art exportation businesses were using questionable receipts, they sent in a team of forensic accountants.

That was like pulling the one loose thread on the sweater of lies. At first the investigators thought they were dealing with only a handful of companies, but each day they tracked down more, often under pseudonyms. Every new receipt they examined seemed to lead to another shell company.

When it added up to 186 different entities, even the accountants were amazed by the enormity of the enterprise. By the time Revenue Canada finally froze all the companies' accounts and the charges were laid, Norman had filed for $5.3 million in GST refunds and received $2.2 million from the federal government over a four-year period.

"It all went too far," Norman says. "I thought it would be a small operation, and then I got others involved and there were more and more companies. I should have stopped long before it came to this."

Norman is proud that in the end it was only he and his brother who were charged. They'd enlisted the aid of several friends to register all the different companies, and as part of the plea arrangement, the accomplices were spared any legal hassles.

"I like to do the right thing," Norman says.

While on probation, Norman continues to work in sales. He's started another company that also seems to be on the ethical borderline. From an office in Laval, Norman is selling long-distance calling plans. The plans aren't as cheap as those currently offered by Bell or any other major long distance company, but Norman says he offers better service.

"It pays the bills right now," he shrugs.

He still dreams of making a name for himself in the business world. There are opportunities in mass marketing, he says, then there is a world of profit to be made by using infomercials on the television to sell products.

"Like I said, I could sell swimming pools to Eskimos. Just give me the chance."

As he smokes another cigarette and drinks the last of his coffee, he is even so bold as to predict another new, but unspecified, venture that will bring him more than $100 million a year in business within the next couple of years.

He does make one promise though: Whatever his next enterprise is, it will have absolutely nothing to do with art or the GST.

IT'S ALL IN THE SWAGGER: THE TALE OF THE LOCKER ROOM BANDIT

Constable Francine St. Laurent was cruising east on Highway 417 when she spotted the Cadillac a few cars ahead of her.

The traffic was fairly heavy that afternoon, the 22nd of April, 1998, but amid the myriad of minivans and Chevy Cavaliers, she couldn't help but notice the luxury car with its metallic paint gleaming in the afternoon sun. As soon as she saw it, there was the twitch, that feeling deep in her spine that something big was about to happen.

The officer maneuvered her police cruiser behind the Cadillac, gliding in slow and easy so as not to spook the driver. She watched as the grey-haired man at the wheel checked his rearview mirror. She let loose a wry smile when he dropped his speed from 115 to 105.

Everyone does that when they see a cop, she laughed to herself. If I wanted to be writing tickets I'd be on the bridge with the radar gun.

She pulled in a bit closer so she could read the blue letters and numbers on the Cadillac's licence plate. 825-TPE. That seemed familiar too. With one eye on the road and the other on her tiny on-board computer, Const. St. Laurent pressed a couple of keys and then typed in the plate number. Out of the corner of her eye, she watched the orange-on-black data screen process her request while ahead of her, the Cadillac signalled and merged into the exit-ramp lane.

For the past two months, Const. St. Laurent and every other cop who worked that end of town had been on the lookout for white Cadillacs. There was a major fraud investigation underway and a white Cadillac was the suspect's ride of choice. The lead detective on the case had come in to brief them during a roll call in February. He told them they were looking for a man named Timothy Clinton, or at least a man who used the name Timothy

Clinton. The detective had received information that the man was living in the city, and he was already wanted on more than 100 Canada-wide warrants. The suspect was a master fraud artist and as the detective showed the picture of Clinton to Const. St. Laurent and the rest of the platoon, he stressed to them that any time they saw a white Cadillac, pull on up beside it and check the face of the driver.

For some reason, the white Cadillac she saw today triggered something. The man in the car had grey hair, no moustache or beard. She remembered that the Timothy Clinton they were looking for was middle-aged and had no facial hair. Then again, she asked herself in a moment of doubt, who else other than a middle-aged man would be driving a white Caddy?

As she watched the Cadillac slow down to take the ramp, the computer screen flashed and coughed up the result of her licence plate search. The car was indeed registered to a Timothy Clinton.

The Caddy took the exit ramp and Const. St. Laurent felt her stomach twist again: This was it. She flipped on her overhead lights, pressed down on the accelerator and sped down the exit ramp after the other car. The man behind the wheel looked startled when he saw the flashing police lights and he brought the Cadillac to a sudden stop at the bottom of the ramp.

Const. St. Laurent stepped out of her police cruiser, hand hovering close to her gun. The driver turned in his seat and looked at her.

Her stomach did a somersault. The face clicked; it was like a thousand flash bulbs going off in her head. This was definitely the suspect.

"Mr. Clinton, I assume?" she asked the driver.

The man's face turned a dismal shade of grey.

The Locker Room Bandit had been busted.

$ $ $

A visit to any big-city courthouse or police station will reveal a very usual range of suspects clogging up the cells and ambling through the corridors.

On the bottom rung, charged with offences like lighting fires or threatening to kill the prime minister, are the NCRs—the Not Criminally Responsibles. They are each messed up in their own particular fashion, but schizophrenia is usually a constant. These particular "accused" are destined for a psychiatric hospital where they will be clinically assessed, found to be incapable of understanding the criminal charges they face, and then be ordered to stay at the hospital or follow a strict diet of medication under constant supervision.

The next level of "accused" caught in the police and court net are the addicts. Crack, cocaine, often heroin, and sometimes just plain old alcohol. The men are caught doing stupid things to feed their addiction, things like breaking into homes and stealing VCRs that they can turn around and sell for $25, enough money to get a quarter gram of cocaine or a couple of rocks of

Theft: The Legalities

CANADIAN CRIMINAL CODE SECTIONS 354, 355

Possession of Property Obtained By Crime

354.(1) Every one commits an offence who has in his possession any property or thing or any proceeds of any property or thing knowing that all or part of the property or thing or the proceeds was obtained by or derived directly or indirectly from

(a) the commission in Canada of an offence punishable by indictment; or

(b) an act or omission anywhere that, if it had occurred in Canada, would have constituted an offence punishable by indictment

Punishment

355.(1) Every one who commits an offence under section 354

(a) is guilty of an indictable offence and liable to imprisonment for a term not exceeding ten years, where the subject-matter of the offence is a testamentary instrument or the value of that subject-matter of the offence exceeds five thousand dollars; or

(b) is guilty

(i) of an indictable offence and liable to imprisonment for a term not exceeding two years; or

(ii) of an offence punishable on summary conviction, where the value of the subject-matter of the offence does not exceed five thousand dollars.

crack if they're a smokehound. One man became so desperate he robbed the same corner store three times in three months. The last time, the store owner even addressed him by name. His take? A couple of cartons of cigarettes each time, and respectively, $262, $191, and $226 from the cash. Every penny went straight to crack and he ended up being sentenced to three years in the penitentiary for that mindless spree.

Then there was the poor sap who got slapped with an 18-month jail sentence for a series of home break-and-enters. From one of the homes, this genius stole a rare penny collection worth more than $15,000. The guy rolled it up into paper coin rolls and cashed it in at the Bank of Montreal for $1.50, all of which went to help secure his next line of the white stuff.

The men are at least better off than the women. They're forced to do the only thing they can do to get the money they need for their heroin or crack: sell their bodies. Every judge has looked into the eyes of some wornout 24-year-old woman with bruises on her arms, ratty second-hand clothes on her body, and a criminal record that already includes seven or eight prostitution charges. What are you going to do? Send her to prison for a couple of months, order her to stay at a halfway home, make sure she gets some drug counselling? That's what every other judge did and still she's back again.

These men and women are regulars at the courthouse or police station, a continuous cycle of addiction and petty crime and drug abuse.

Above the addicts are the "rounders." These are the guys who've been around the system for years and have criminal records filled with assault, b-and-e, drug possession, and theft charges. They know the game, have the phone number of their favourite criminal lawyer memorized, and are usually prepared to do their time if they've done the crime. One guy got busted stealing lobsters from a grocery store one week, then liquor bottles from the LCBO the next. Another rounder got picked up for backing a pick-up truck up to somebody else's boat and driving off with it.

Rounders have done crime their whole lives and simply don't know any better. They laugh with the prison guards and crack jokes to their lawyers. They also know the code. These are the guys who would never rat out one of their own. Maybe they'll drop the name of some punk drug dealer who's working out of the apartment two floors down from them, do the cops a small favour like that, but the average rounder would rather lose a leg than testify on the stand.

Next you have the gangs or the guys who think they have the balls and the brains to pull a couple of serious gun jobs. The street gangs deal drugs or steal cars or send women out to work the corners. They come up with fanciful names like Ace Crew or the Corner Boys and run a couple of city blocks for a while before their violence and stupidity get them taken down. Then they run through the system. With their long young-offender records and penchant for violence, they know they're looking at a long visit to the Kingston Penitentiary or some other maximum security facility.

As for the ones who come up with a plan to rob a couple of grocery stores or walk into a bank with a gun, these are the guys who are just starting to get desperate. In a couple of years they'll be the addicts, but for now their drugs, gambling, and partying are just a way of life and they don't mind pulling a bank job to keep that life going. When these guys get popped by police, they also know they're facing serious time. The guys who put on balaclavas and rushed into grocery stores, jumped on the counter and stuck shotguns in the faces of cashiers each got hit with sentences of between seven and ten years.

```
CANADIAN CRIMINAL CODE, SECTION 342

Theft, Forgery, Etc. of Credit Card

342.(1) Everyone who

    (a) steals a credit card

    (b) forges or falsifies a credit card

    (c) has in his possession, uses or deals in any
        other way with a credit card that he knows
        was obtained

        (i) by the commission in Canada of an offence,
            or

        (ii)by an act or omission anywhere that, if
            it had occurred in Canada, would have
            constituted an offence, or

    (d) uses a credit card that he knows has been
        revoked or cancelled is guilty of

    (e) an indictable offence and is liable to
        imprisonment for a term not exceeding ten
        years, or

    (f) an offence punishable on summary conviction
```

These types of "accused" are treated warily by police and court staff, and in general keep up such a tough front that they muster up their most menacing look for the moment when the judge walks into the courtroom. The middle class make frequent visits to the courthouse or cop shop as well, but mostly with an expensive lawyer in tow and a drinking and driving charge they're trying to quash. Once in a while they show up in domestic court for punching their wives or are charged with some sort of sexual perversion like possession of child pornography. A lot of older folks are teetering through the courthouse these days too, charged with sexually assaulting their daughters or nephews or students decades ago.

Then there are the murders and attempted murders. These people represent the whole spectrum of society, from an upper-class woman who kills her husband to a drug lord who settles a cocaine debt with a gun to a bar fighter who needed a knife to end that night's battle.

But among this constant flow of psychiatric cases, ragged addicts, gangster hoods, sex perverts, wife-beaters, drunk drivers and stone killers, there sometimes comes a more polished rock, a soul who has devoted considerable time, energy, and thought to the pursuit of crime. These cases are rare indeed and they're the type that involve such daring or persistence or ingenuity that they make headlines across the country.

The Locker Room Bandit was one of these cases.

$ $ $

Timothy Clinton is in fact a silver-haired, lightning-tongued man named Ken who has been playing the fraud game for more than thirty years.

He was fifty-six years old the day he got pulled over by Const. St. Laurent, but that was hardly his first brush with police. His criminal record dates back to the first half of 1958 when he was just sixteen. Since then he has amassed a string of convictions for fraud, theft, assault, and other petty offences. By the time he was released from his latest stay in prison in Vancouver in the early 1990s, Ken had been working angles on frauds for decades and figured he pretty well knew every trick in the book.

The first key to the fraud game is appearance. Dress for success. You are what you wear. Looks are everything. Ken lived all those maxims. He kept his grey hair short and sharp-looking with bi-weekly visits to the hair stylist. A monthly facial kept his skin soft and healthy, while regular manicures kept his hands in top condition. His suits were strictly double-breasted Harry Rosen specials that shouted success and wealth. And on his wrist he always wore a trademark gold Gucci watch. Walking down a busy street with his shoes polished and his briefcase at his side, he looked every bit the bank vice-president or director of marketing for a software firm. Certainly nothing like the experienced criminal he was.

The next factor was swagger and charm. In this business, you had to be confident when pulling a job. You had to look people in the eye and take control of everything, because the truth was, you were taking something that wasn't yours. Being a little bit of a flirt doesn't hinder you either; Ken always had a good line for a cashier or bank teller. He was so charming, detectives still chortle about the time he managed to seduce his own parole officer.

The last thing was the hook. You could be as clever as you wanted, you could look like you just stepped out of the pages of the damn Harry Rosen catalogue, but if you didn't have a good angle, you might as well be flipping burgers at the local Wendy's.

There are dozens of fraud schemes, each requiring a different degree of brashness and amorality. But a few are so well thought out that they border on inspiration.

There are the telephone frauds based out of Montreal and Calgary, the operations where teams of telemarketers call people at home with the news that they've won a big cash prize or brand new car. Of course, the lucky winner will have to send off a couple hundred dollars to cover taxes or shipping or some other expense. The winners send off the money and never see their prizes. These setups can earn millions before police shut them down.

Or there's the old favourite, the "internal bank investigation" fraud. A man will call some unsuspecting citizen at home and explain that he works with a bank's internal security service. They suspect an employee of stealing funds, the man says, and they need the good citizen's cooperation to help catch that employee. What they want the person to do is transfer funds from a personal account to a special numbered account at a pre-set time the next morning. The man on the phone says that the suspect employee will be working at that time and they expect to catch him or her skimming off the transfer.

The voice on the phone assures the person that the funds will be returned in full a few minutes after they have caught the dishonest employee in the act. Instead, immediately after the funds have been transferred, the man who was posing as a member of the fictitious bank security team scoops the money out of the numbered account, never to be seen again.

Then there are the regular range of welfare frauds, or cheque frauds, or insurance frauds, the things that keep police busy and that every half-bit con artist knows how to perpetrate. All of these schemes are tried time and time again and are often successful, at least for a little while. But they aren't truly inspired.

When Ken got out of prison, he swore he was done with crime. He wanted to go straight, to get a job or go back to school. For a couple of months he tried at least, but he couldn't crack the Vancouver job market. His only real skill was an old apprenticeship he'd taken in tool-and-die making, and in the early '90s there simply wasn't much demand for a middle-aged tool-and-die maker with a criminal record as long as Ken's. He thought about going back to school to get more training, but when he ran into difficulties with his student loan applications, he became frustrated.

After a few months like that, Ken did pretty much the only thing he could think of. He decided to go back to crime. He already knew about the look and the charm, of course. The thing was, he wanted a new angle, a better angle, an *inspired* angle. Something that hadn't been tried before, and something that could net him a lot of easy cash.

The idea hit him a couple of months after being released. He'd gone to a gym in downtown Vancouver one morning for a quick workout. As he was sitting in the locker room after his final stint on the treadmill, he couldn't help but notice the rush of men in business suits who flooded the gym at noon to squeeze a workout into their day. As he watched them jostle around the locker room, Ken could sense the money oozing from their pores. These were rich men. It was at that moment the idea struck.

Ken went home with his head ablaze as he tried to work out the various risks and pitfalls in his new plan. By the next morning, he was sure he had a scheme that would net him more than enough money to keep him living in style.

$ $ $

The first thing Ken did when he arrived in a new city was pick up a copy of the Yellow Pages and a local map. He would tear out the page of the telephone book with the listings for the health clubs and then drive around the town, checking out the location of each club and estimating how rich its patrons would be. Over the years, he'd picked up preferences for certain chains of health clubs that catered to wealthy clients. Good Life fitness clubs were his absolute favourite, but a downtown YMCA or independent gym could be just as profitable for him.

Once he found a club he liked, he parked his car, usually the Cadillac, and then walked into the reception area shortly before noon. He always wore an expensive suit and carried a special duffel bag. At the front desk, he'd launch into his spiel.

"Hi," he'd say warmly to the young man or woman behind the counter. "I was wondering if you offered day passes. I've been transferred to the area and I've been looking for a new gym. I was hoping I could check out your facilities."

After more idle conversation, Ken would either be given a free day pass or be asked to buy one for five dollars. Sometimes, if it wasn't too busy, the staff even found the time to give him a brief tour. Inevitably, Ken found himself in the locker room just as the club was hit with its noontime rush. He sat there on one of the benches, slowly staking off his shoes and jacket, watching every face that came in. Who looked like they had money? More important, who looked like they had money *and* looked a little bit like him? Considering how many middle-aged businessmen in suits swarmed into the average health club at lunch, it never took Ken long to find his mark.

As he sat on his bench, watching his target change into gym clothes, Ken prepared to move. He slipped his shoes back on and got up to get his jacket. When his target finally closed and locked his locker, Ken was on his feet. First, he followed the other man to the gym area to make sure he was safely starting his workout. Then, it was back to the target's locker.

Inside Ken's special duffel bag, he kept three pairs of mini bolt cutters. With a quick glance to make sure nobody was watching, Ken pulled out a pair and neatly clipped off his victim's lock. Then he went through the man's pockets, looking for his wallet and other ID. Sometimes the other man had stuffed the wallet into his shoe, as if that were one last line of defence against somebody like Ken.

Once the wallet and identification were located, Ken slipped them out of the locker and into his pocket. Then, Ken opened his duffel bag where he had dozens of brand new locks, a couple each of every brand on the market—Dudley, Master, the whole selection. Ken would quickly match the victim's lock to a new one in his bag and replace the clipped lock with an identical twin.

This was a brilliant move. Assuming the man inside was going to work out for at least half an hour, that alone gave Ken a 30-minute head start. Then, when the victim came back to his locker and tried his combination, it wouldn't work. The victim would never immediately suspect foul play; instead he would assume his lock was broken or he'd forgotten the combination. He'd then go search out a club employee and get the lock cut off. Only then, when he looked for his wallet, would he realize he'd been ripped off.

This whole routine usually took at least another 15 minutes, usually 20. That meant Ken had a good 45 minutes alone with the man's wallet and identification before a single alarm bell was sounded. And Ken put every minute of that time to good use.

Walking out of the club, he'd give the attendant at the desk a quick wave and promise to see them again soon. Then it'd be out the door, into the car, and full-speed ahead to the nearest branch of his victim's bank—making sure, of course, it wasn't the other man's "home" branch where the staff would recognize him.

With a wallet full of ID, including bank cards and credit cards, Ken had everything he needed to clean out the other man's accounts. Using his considerable charm, he'd go to a teller and explain that he needed a cash advance on the credit card and the balance on his savings account. Sometimes he'd say he'd forgotten the PIN code for his bank card, create a new one, and then empty the accounts through an automated teller.

Some identification? Sure, said Ken, pulling out a driver's licence, a health card and whatever else the man from the gym might have had in his wallet. The teller would usually glance at the picture and then at Ken—greyish hair, white, middle-aged, just like the picture on the ID—it was always close enough for any teller. The fact that Ken was dressed in his expensive suit, had a flashy Gucci on his wrist, and handed over the cards with hands that had recently been treated to a manicure helped ease whatever other concerns the teller might have. It was simple: Everyone has a stereotypical image of a thief, and Ken didn't fit that image.

In about ten minutes, Ken would have gotten two or three thousand dollars in cash advances from the credit cards along with whatever else was in the man's savings or checking accounts.

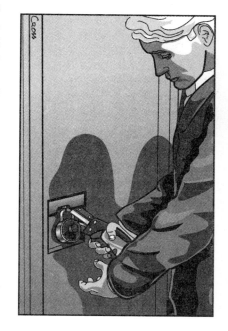

"Buying a used car for my son," he might explain on one occasion. "I need to pay in cash." Or another time it might be a new deck on the back of his house. "The carpenter wants to be paid in cash," Ken would say with a shrug as the teller counted out the hundred-dollar bills.

With a couple of forged signatures and another wave, Ken was gone. Back out to his car, back out on the highway, usually about the same time his victim was fruitlessly trying to open his combination lock back at the gym. Ken would be out of town before the lock was cut and the wallet declared missing. By the time the banks and credit card companies had been notified, he was likely in another city, looking at another set of Yellow Pages and planning his score for the next day.

For Ken, or the Locker Room Bandit as he soon became known, his new scheme was incredibly profitable. Sometimes he would walk out of a bank with as much as $9,000 or $10,000 in cash. Other times it would only be $2,000 or $3,000. But the bottom line was always good. For a couple of hours' work and a little bit of boldness, he was rewarded with a healthy payday.

$ $ $

Ken began his spree of locker room thefts in 1992 and continued full tilt for six years. On average he pulled a job or two a week, making hundreds of scores overall. He'd pulled locker room robberies across Canada—in Vancouver, Calgary, Toronto, Ottawa, Windsor, London, any place there was a couple of health clubs and enough people so he could blend in as just another businessman.

The secret was road trips. He'd take his Cadillac out, drive across the province once or twice a month and hit different cities each time. He had to pay a lot in gas and hotel rooms, but these were minor costs compared to the bounties that awaited him; police estimate that during his career as the Locker Room Bandit, Ken took home more than $1-million in ill-gotten cash.

The amazing thing is that, for most of the time, he did it with the police knowing exactly who the Locker Room Bandit was. With his long criminal record, Ken's fingerprints were on file across Canada, and it didn't take long for police to pick up his trail by dusting the lockers he hit and the bank papers he signed. At one point, there were more than a hundred different warrants out for his arrest, each one issued for a different locker room heist.

But even though the police knew who was doing the crime, there was still one big question: Where was he? Ken had started out in Vancouver and then moved to Ontario halfway through his spree. He usually lived with women and always under an assumed name like Timothy Clinton. Locker room after locker room was hit and police knew Ken was doing it. They just didn't know where they could find him.

Their first break came in January 1998. As Ken was pulling out of a bank parking lot in London, a suspicious teller had jotted down his licence plate number just to be on the safe side—something about Ken had seemed fishy. The teller's instincts were justified a couple of hours later when the police arrived and started to ask questions about a man who'd made a massive cash withdrawal. The teller slipped the officer the licence plate number, and the hunt for the Locker Room Bandit was on.

The plate was registered to a Timothy Clinton. Police went to the address connected to the licence plate, but it turned out to be nothing more than a postal box rented from a MoneyMart outlet. As it happened, this Timothy Clinton had been in a couple of days before to rent the box for another year. The clerk at the MoneyMart remembered him; he'd paid with a hundred-dollar bill and wore a gold Gucci watch. Police pulled out the old mugshots of Ken from when he'd been arrested in Vancouver almost ten years before. Dead match. The police now knew what city the Locker Room Bandit lived in and what name he lived under.

Oddly enough, the real Timothy Clinton was actually one of Ken's previous victims. A professor at the University of Calgary, the real Timothy Clinton had gone to the campus gym one lunch hour for a workout. When he came back, he couldn't open his lock and then found his wallet missing. In this case, not only had the Locker Room Bandit struck, but he'd stolen an identity as well.

This added a new twist for the police investigators. When they called the real Timothy Clinton, they found out he visited Toronto for business all the time. Yet police in Ontario had a province-wide warrant for Timothy Clinton's arrest. What if the real Timothy Clinton got stopped in a routine traffic stop? Investigators gave Professor Clinton their pager numbers and told him to call immediately if he got caught in one of the traps they'd set for the fake Timothy Clinton.

Soon after they put the province-wide bulletin out for Timothy Clinton, investigators caught another break. A Toronto police source told them that a Timothy Clinton stayed at the Westin Hotel in Toronto two days a month. Some background research proved it was Ken, the Locker Room Bandit. Police told hotel staff to alert them the second Ken walked in and gave them his fake Timothy Clinton identification.

It looked like a sure thing, but as always, there was one thing they didn't count on. Ken had always been a big tipper, dropping twenties at the hotel like confetti. Someone at the Westin remembered that and thought they'd repay him by letting him know the police were looking for him. Ken never returned to the Westin.

That left the white Cadillac with licence plate 825-TPE.

For weeks, investigators were tracing every white Cadillac, telling the officers on the road to do the same thing. Then, finally, on April 22, 1998, Const. St. Laurent came across the white Cadillac on Highway 417.

Ken argued for a while, but once the fingerprints came back, there was no point. He had to get himself a lawyer.

$ $ $

When they searched Ken's house, police found 103 wallets. Then there were the IDs of dozens of other victims, bolt cutters, pages of telephone listings for health clubs, and city maps. Add in the fingerprints they had from dozens of crime scenes, and Ken realized the cops had a pretty good case against him. He did the only logical thing. He agreed to plead guilty.

As soon as he was in custody, police forces across the country began laying fraud charges against him. When it was all said and done, Ken faced close to 300 separate charges. He made a deal to plead guilty to them all in one shot, saving the courts tens of thousands of dollars in trial costs. In return, he was given a three-and-a-half-year sentence in the penitentiary for his million-dollar crime spree.

When the case was finally concluded in the spring of 1999, Justice Paul Belanger listened intently to all the crimes the Locker Room Bandit had committed.

"If you have a talent, it is as a talented crook," the judge told him afterwards. "But not that talented, bearing in mind where you currently sit."

Sitting in the prisoner's box, Ken did the only thing he could do. He nodded his head and kept his eyes on the floor.

WHIPPING UP SOME BUSINESS: DOMINATING MEN FOR MONEY

How was she supposed to know? *Really.*

When he spoke on the phone, he spoke as any new client would. He was shy and hesitant, always speaking around the services offered. They talked only in general terms, discussing his interest in experimentation and his desire to broaden his sexual horizons. She asked him about himself and he told her he was in human resources and lived outside of town. Probably the truth, she guessed. He gave his name as Richard. That was probably a lie.

After five minutes, he became nervous with how pointed the questions had become and hung up. She knew he would call again. Eight years in the business had taught her that much.

Two days later he did call back and asked her if she remembered him. Yes, Richard, she said. Of course I remember you. I'm very good with voices.

He was a little more comfortable now, a little more forward. He explained to her that he was very much in love with his girlfriend, but something was lacking. There were dark fantasies that wouldn't leave him and he wanted to be able to act them out. I don't think there's any point living a sexual lie, he said. I don't want to spend my life wondering "What if?"

She agreed completely and told him he was free to come by for a visit, to talk this out in person. The fee was $200 for the introductory session, mind you, and the first session was nothing but a conversation to see if they were compatible. Would that be all right? Richard agreed and the session was scheduled for the following week.

She worked out of her home. The house was a ranch-style bungalow tucked inside a quiet, working class neighbourhood a 20-minute drive north of downtown. There were polished wood floors and Persian rugs so thick that when you wore bare feet it felt like you were sinking in up to your ankles. The house was sparsely decorated with comfortable furniture, especially the living room: an overstuffed couch, a beautiful old wicker chair for reading, polished wood book cases all around. The introductory sessions were always held in the living room, with the couch and the chair and a wide picture window that let you watch the neighbourhood unfold.

The maid had been there the day before Richard's appointment, so when he arrived the house still smelled of Pine Sol and Mr. Clean. They sat and talked about the garden and the weather and the books in the book cases and anything else Richard could think of to avoid the specific reason for his visit. She poured him a glass of white wine to calm his nerves, and finally, he began to talk about what he wanted.

He wasn't gay, he said. There was his girlfriend and he had always been with women. It was just that some nagging part of him, something deep inside, had always fantasized about being . . . Richard became embarrassed again and got up to leave.

She reached over and put a comforting hand on his forearm and told him everything was all right here. He was safe with her. No one would judge him, no one would laugh at him. Human sexuality was complex and mysterious. One of the most important things we can do is try to understand what drives it, she told Richard.

Richard sat back down. He was an average-looking man with dark hair cut short and a chin that betrayed a five o'clock shadow even though it was barely past noon. Today he was wearing a navy blue business suit with a crisp white shirt and red silk tie flecked with gold. His black dress shoes sparkled from a recent polishing. She went to the kitchen and got the bottle of wine from the refrigerator. He graciously accepted another glass.

I've always wanted to be on the other end, he said. I don't know how to explain it. It's just something I can't stop thinking about.

She nodded and smiled. Over the years, she had been around enough men and serviced enough more to know all the code words and euphemisms. She easily guessed what he was talking about.

You want to be taken like a woman is taken? she asked. She purposely kept the terms vague, knowing that he himself had not yet come to terms with what it was he wanted. Richard nodded. Yes. Something like that. She smiled and reached for his forearm again. It's healthy to explore this, she assured him.

After another ten minutes of conversation, she had a complete grasp of what Richard so desperately craved. It was actually a relatively common request in her line of work. He wanted to be taken from behind. He wanted to submit to the indignities he imagined he submitted women to. He wanted anal sex but he didn't want to be with a man. He wanted to be with a woman acting as a man while he acted as a woman.

She told him that it wouldn't be a problem, that it could all be arranged. A mixture of relief and fear passed over Richard's face. It was a look she'd seen on a hundred men when they realized their fantasy could become a reality. The cost would be $400 a session, she explained to him as they walked to the door. I won't take any appointments right now. After you've thought about it, if you still want to see me again, call. And, Richard, she added, cleanliness is very important. I expect you to be clean and showered if you do come

The Legalities

CANADIAN CRIMINAL CODE, KEEPING A COMMON BAWDY HOUSE

210. (1) Every one who keeps a common bawdy-house is guilty of an indictable offence and liable to imprisonment for a term not exceeding two years.

(Common bawdy-house—any defined space is capable of being a common bawdy house, even a parking lot, if there is localization of acts of prostitution within its specified boundaries. However, mere presence by prostitutes in the parking lot on a number of occasions... is not sufficient to establish them as keeping a bawdy house.)

CANADIAN CRIMINAL CODE, OFFENCE IN RELATION TO PROSTITUTION

213. (1) Every person who, in a public place or in any place open to public view

    (a) stops or attempts to stop any motor vehicle

    (b) impedes the free flow of pedestrian or vehicular traffic or ingress and egress from premises adjacent to that place; or

    (c) stops or attempts to stop any person or in any manner communicates or attempts to communicate with any person

for the purpose of engaging in prostitution or of obtaining the sexual services of a prostitute is guilty of an offence punishable on summary conviction.

back to see me. If you are serious about this, you'll have to be open to an enema as well, she warned.

He nodded agreement and walked to his silver Volvo parked in her driveway.

$ $ $

They were always a bit surprised by the first session. Some expected her to answer the door wearing a leather mask and brandishing a whip. Others thought she would be a vampish porn star, all cleavage and thigh, like they'd seen in magazines or on the Internet. Instead, she always dressed conservatively for the first session. A business suit was her preference, something neutral and pleasant, usually greys and beiges. She chose a grey suit with modest heels for her first meeting with Richard.

Her size startled men too, though it quickly became a selling point. She was a large woman, a touch over six feet tall, with auburn hair that just brushed her wide shoulders. She had full lips and high cheekbones, a memento of her Scandinavian grandmother. One of her eyes was on the lazy side, which always kept her guests wondering exactly where she was looking. In her mind, that was another advantage.

They were also surprised by her house. Stuck in a family neighbourhood, decorated like something out of *House and Garden*, it was nothing like they imagined. Men believe that a dominatrix must live in a raw downtown apartment or a gothic old home with a wrought-iron fence. Not smack dab in the middle of suburbia with Chrysler minivans patrolling the streets and Fisher Price toys scattered across the lawns.

It wasn't an accident that she presented herself this way. She'd learned long ago that you had to be careful in this type of business. Some men couldn't reign their dark impulses so you had to be cautious. By shrouding herself in normalcy, she thought it helped protect her from the abnormal. At least until she was ready for it.

The first step in the screening process was the phone call. When she first started in the early '90s, she was naïve. She thought everybody who called had a good side and that even if things got out of control, she could handle it. Then she learned about the perverts and the police. The perverts were the ones who wanted to act like little girls or re-enact violent rape scenes. They weren't healthy. She'd always tabbed them as pedophiles and rapists, or at the very least, pedophiles and rapists waiting to happen.

Then there were the police. Who knew when some puritanical officer would make it his goal to rid the community of so-called sexual deviants? They would call up now and again, asking pointed cop-like questions such as, "How much to fuck?"

After a couple of years, she found she could weed out most of these types through the first phone call. She listened to their voice, paid attention to their mannerisms, and asked questions about their sexuality and past experiences. If she didn't like the answers she was getting, she told them they'd made a mistake by calling her and please, never call again.

However, if they were like Richard, pleasant and nervous, they were probably first-timers and not very dangerous. Likewise, if they knew exactly what they were looking for, spoke in specifics about house rules or becoming a slave, they were probably old hands at hiring a dominatrix and again, were likely not to be much trouble. In cases like this, where her instincts told her everything was safe, she invited them over for a conversation and nothing more. The price tag of $200 would scare off anybody who wasn't serious and the face-to-face conversation would let her know if her instincts about the prospective client were true.

She chose to wear the conservative clothes and meet in the living room to keep things neutral. They could talk without distraction and she could look into a man's eyes while they weren't clouded with sexual frenzy. After sharing a cup of tea or a glass of wine together in her living room, if the man still seemed right and decent, then she would agree to another meeting. At this meeting, they would begin to work on the fantasies the man had so haltingly articulated on the phone and in her living room. They would also talk about the house rules and the behaviour expected from her clients.

Of course, the second meeting took place in her basement dungeon.

$ $ $

The basement was down a set of stairs in the kitchen. She always kept the door closed and locked when she had friends or company over. Many did not know what she did for a living; she simply told most she was a therapist. It would be uncomfortable for everyone if a friend went exploring or in search of a hammer and stumbled into the dungeon. Too shocking to those unfamiliar with such arrangements.

The basement was finished, but the walls were all covered in black cloth and the floor was made up of grey linoleum tiles. There was a six-by-six steel cage in one corner for men who needed to be locked up. On one wall was a wooden rack, much like the ones that hold cues in pool halls. But her rack held rows of black leather whips, dangling lengths of silver metal chain, and restraints for the hands and feet. Most of it, she admits, is only for show; in her business, there tends to be a lot of show.

On another wall there is a shelf with three leather masks with fierce eye holes, each zipped onto a Styrofoam head. Beside the heads was a row of intimidating dildos and vibrators, some looking like replicas of ogre-sized penises. There were also two pairs of plain, old-fashioned handcuffs. She had some more expensive leather cuffs with fur lining, but they snapped a couple of months ago, she says. The centrepiece of the room is the enormous, four-post bed. It is fixed with latex sheets and manacles that hang from each of the sturdy posts.

Once she is in this room, her countenance and appearance change. Instead of the grey business suit, she wears more outrageous attire: a black leather cat suit, leather boots and often a mask. In this room, she is in control and expects each one of her orders to be obeyed.

Richard called back three days after drinking white wine in her living room. This was a bit of a surprise; she'd guessed he would be on the phone to her in less than 24 hours. She thought she saw it in his eyes. No matter, when Richard did phone, there was an appointment open later that week, so he gladly booked it. It was her policy to never take more than one session a day, she explained. It was too emotionally draining for her and the second client never got what he deserved.

$ $ $

Richard arrived at 2 p.m. sharp and this time she met him wearing her black leather cat-suit. It clung tight to her body, accentuating every curve and nuance of flesh. She also wore knee-high red leather boots and elbow-high leather gloves. You could tell it shocked Richard a little, but not in a bad way.

This time she wasn't nearly as cordial upon greeting him. She told him to follow her and led him down to the basement.

She'd prepared specially for him, displaying a selection of strap-on dildos along one of the shelves. There were two pairs of tight Spandex shorts with dildos attached to the crotch area; one of the dildos was slim and four inches long and the other a bit thicker and six inches long. She could slip these on and be able to handle a reasonable facsimile of an erect penis. The problem with the slip-on shorts was that because the Spandex wasn't as tight as it could be, the penis didn't stay in one place. It just flopped about, so while working she had to hold it in place with one hand. It could be a bit of a momentum breaker, she found.

She also had two strap-on dildos, each of which had three adjustable, leather straps, one that went between her legs and the other two which circled around her waist. They buckled in the back and each of these straps could

Most dominas craft their businesses to skirt prostitution laws. Among the tricks is asking for a "gratuity" instead of setting an hourly rate and insisting on staying fully clothed during the sessions. What follows are the "House Rules" of one who calls herself Mistress K:

House Rules

1. A gift shows sincerity as well as appreciation.

2. Unless you have something to offer—a service or a skill, Mistress K is not looking for personal slaves.

3. Mistress K does not go nude or topless during the sessions.

4. Mistress K does not switch, so do not ask her to be submissive.

5. Mistress K does not engage in any type of sexual activities with her submissives. The only body worship she does is boot and foot.

6. Mistress K accepts submissives of all races, sexes, and ages (18 and up).

7. Mistress K hates last-minute scrounging. If you are going to be seen by her, it is mandatory you have the previously discussed gratuity.

8. Mistress K loathes submissives who have not taken proper hygiene measures. If you request dildo training, you will be required to be thoroughly cleansed via an enema.

9. Mistress K does not tolerate any sexism, racism or machismo.

10. Mistress K demands respect from the moment you call her to the moment you see her to the moment you walk out the door.

11. Mistress K does not allow second chances. If you screw up once, you will be banished.

12. Mistress K does not care if you have a Ph.D. in nuclear physics, or if you wash bottles for a living, She treats all her submissives the same way.

13. Mistress K demands that if you are going to be late for a session or cancel, you notify her ASAP. No-shows will not be granted another session.

be tightened to the point where the dildo penis would stand firmly in one place. Much more convenient. The dildos on these two were also of different sizes; one was a thin six-inch member and the other was a much thicker, much longer, 10-inch version.

There was never any physical contact the first time she brought clients into the dungeon. Rarely was there ever physical contact on the second or third visits either. She wanted to make sure they were ready first. She wanted them to be so vulnerable, so desperate, so eager that they would tell her exactly what they wanted her to do to them.

It was all about training, training the new clients how to accept orders and training them to accept punishment when they didn't follow those orders. She also didn't allow physical contact because she wanted to clearly demonstrate she was in control. After the first couple of hours, the men craved contact, begged for it, even cried for it. At that point, they were completely hers.

After the years she'd spent in the business, she'd learned that the men who wanted a domination service were almost always successful, intelligent and in positions of power or authority. They were also almost always white. They tended to be men who gave orders and made big decisions and had to carry the stress of it with them 24 hours a day. These men didn't want to be in control any more. That, combined with dark, repressed fantasies of anal sex, or whipping, or humiliation would draw them to her.

She was sure Richard fell into this category. If she was to imagine a human resources executive it would be Richard with his conservative suits and ingratiating smile. As he walked into the basement, his eyes widened. When he saw the strap-on dildos his eyes widened even more.

"How much did you say the session was?"

That was the sign. She should've known then. If she'd had her wits about her, she would've known. It was too forward. It didn't fit.

Instead, she answered, "$400. You can leave it on the shelf."

Richard pulled out his wallet and put the money on the table. Then he pulled out the badge. "I'm with the police. I'm going to have to take you in."

Just like that, she was charged with keeping a common bawdy house. He'd seemed so innocent, so needy, just like any of the other men who walked through her door and down into her dungeon. Richard was a cop.

How was she supposed to know? *Really.*

$ $ $

Nobody grows up thinking they're going to work in the sex trade. You imagine becoming a nurse or a teacher or an airline stewardess. You dress up as a bride on Halloween and like all the other girls, you wait with anxiety clawing at your stomach to see how many boys send you sloppy K-Mart cards on Valentine's Day.

It didn't help that she was so shy to begin with, so painfully shy she often wouldn't speak at school for weeks at a time. When she started to grow, it made it even worse. She was always a tall girl, but her growth spurt came a little earlier than everyone else's and lasted a little longer. By Grade 5 she was taller than any boy in the class, and the only Valentine's Day cards she received were the ones she sent to herself.

Her mom lived in the suburbs, in the house that her father had lost in the divorce. She didn't fit in at the local high school where the boys wanted to be hockey stars and the girls wanted to marry hockey stars. She left school shortly after Grade 10 started, never telling anybody—not that anybody cared. Her dad had moved to another city. Her mom was working every day and out with a new boyfriend every night. It was easy to intercept the phone calls from the school and fake the signatures when needed. She spent her days reading and walking around the neighbourhood.

Her virginity was lost at 16 to the man next door. He called her over while she was on one of her walks. His wife was at work and he'd taken the week off to install a new fence in the backyard. He gave her a light beer and then took her to the guest bedroom. It was rough and painful but she went back when he waved to her the next day and the day after that.

The neighbourhood was small and boring with everybody at work or in school. It seemed natural that she start taking the bus downtown during the days, and more natural still to get a job to fill her time. A manager who couldn't stop looking at her breasts gave her a job serving tables at an English-style pub. She was still only 17, but the manager didn't even bother to ask. After a while it seemed inconvenient to make the bus ride home every night, so she moved in with one of the other waitresses and truth be told, her mother didn't miss her at all.

It was a nice change from high school to have men pay attention to her at the pub. They didn't mind her height or her quiet nature. In return for that kindness, she didn't mind accompanying them home at the end of her shift. Her shyness didn't bother any of them, for she quickly realized all men loved to talk and a quiet woman was like a confessional.

She learned so much about men that way—how some could be so strong in the pub but so meek at home and others would look so quiet sipping their beer yet become so forceful and angry back in their apartments. For her it didn't really make a difference though; she seemed to be able to make them all happy.

WHIPPING UP SOME BUSINESS

She worked downtown like this for ten years, waiting tables at different pubs and restaurants, drifting from man to man. It became easy to predict how a man would be and what he would want from her. It was almost a game, and with each man she changed her role, molding herself to his desires. They often came back again, wanted dinner or a movie or a walk along the lake. She never saw any point to this, so she politely declined. When some became desperate, she would walk away to avoid a scene.

It surprised her the first time somebody offered her money, and she hastily refused. Later that night, she kicked herself for that. She could've used the extra hundred dollars.

It was apparent to her that she attracted a certain type of man, the kind of man who, the worse you treated him, the happier he was. She decided part of it was her intimidating height and part of it was her aloof acceptance of their desires. Looking back, she can't even remember the first time she used handcuffs on a man or brought a whip into bed. Someone must have asked her to; she certainly never would've thought of it on her own. There was a vague recollection of the absolute gratitude the man had shown her afterwards. Maybe that's what planted the seed? It's hard to know, but it was easy to build up a collection of these sexual aids: handcuffs, vibrators, anal beads, or whatever else a man suggested or hinted at. After a while, it seemed natural to keep pushing the edge and the men she was with always yearned for more.

It was 1990 when she quit waitressing. At 32, she felt she was getting too old to work in bars. The smoke was making her sick and though the faces changed, it all seemed the same. She didn't work for months after that, so it became necessary to accept a gift now and again from some of her lovers. They all told her they'd never met a woman like her, a woman who knew exactly what they wanted.

It was one of these men who gave her the suggestion. He'd been seeing a dominatrix for years. He told her it cost him $200 for a single visit and there wasn't even sex involved. It's nothing compared to you, he told her, and I don't even have to pay you.

It made her think. Why go back to work? She liked having these relationships with men so why not get something tangible in return. She bought a sexual encyclopedia and read it from cover-to-cover in three days, absorbing every detail. Much of it she'd already learned first-hand, some of it was new, but none of it made her uncomfortable.

It took nerve to place her first ad, and she used a fake name of course. Mistress Alexandra. It was as good as any. It only cost her $30 a week in the local alternative weekly so it wasn't exactly a huge financial risk.

Thinking back, it was like turning on a faucet; the calls just came gushing in. Sure, there were a lot from drunk frat boys and horny 14-year-olds, but there were also a lot of grown men with real money in their wallets. It was no different than what happened in the bars when she was a waitress. Except now, instead of flirting face-to-face, she flirted over the phone. And when they left, she was a couple of hundred dollars richer.

She didn't like to admit it, but early on she was really no different than a prostitute with whips and handcuffs. But over the years, she read more about domination and became more familiar with the psychological side of what she was doing. She started putting up more barriers between her clients and herself, focussing more on the emotional stimulation than the physical.

During all that time, she kept a detailed ledger and Richard had been her 184th client in nine years. It sounded like a lot, but most had only visited two or three times and then given up or gone in search of greater fulfillment.

There had been bad moments, when men confessed to decades-old crimes or broke down into wild, sobbing anguish when the reality of their desires became too much to bear. But as she thumbed through that well-worn ledger, she realized it had almost all been good. She took four or five appointments a week, which gave her more than enough money for rent and a car and vacations. She had a half-dozen clients she had been seeing for more than five years, steady, long-term relationships.

And though she had to deal with her share of perverts and vice cops, she had never been beaten and never been charged. At least not until Richard came into her life.

$ $ $

The police charged her with running a common bawdy house, the legal term for a house of prostitution. If she wasn't so stubborn, she would've simply pleaded guilty and gotten it over and done with. The lawyer she spoke to told her all she would face was a fine, perhaps $1,000, maybe less. After all, she had no criminal record and it wasn't as if she was public enemy number one.

But she couldn't let herself. The embarrassment and humiliation of being arrested and fingerprinted quickly turned to anger. The look in the eyes of the police officers had stuck with her. Completely condescending. They looked at her as if she was an animal or some sick sexual pervert. She boiled inside at that. What they were doing to her was wrong. She was hurting nobody, the neighbours never complained, and she offered a valuable service at a fair price. Yet these arrogant officers came into her home and treated her like a criminal. She was a good person. She'd volunteered in a rape crisis centre in the past. She regularly donated money to the shelter for victims of domestic violence. She bought Girl Guide cookies, for Christ's sake.

There was so much more evil in the world. She'd seen the stories in the newspaper and on television about the pedophiles and the child pornography. She'd had a friend who had his head split open as he left a bank machine. Yet despite all of that, the police spent their time arresting *her*. Never in her life had she really taken a stand for anything and she knew it wasn't a wise thing to do now, but she couldn't help herself. This was simply ludicrous and she was confident a judge would agree.

Her lawyer warned her the chances weren't good. No judge was likely to break new ground by declaring a dominatrix a legal businesswoman. It was prostitution in the eyes of most and she was trapped in a legal system that chose to punish the women who ventured down that avenue to earn money.

The first day she walked into the courthouse, she became a spectacle. She wore her grey business suit, the same suit she'd chosen to meet Richard in that first day. She also wore thick high heels that brought her to well over six foot four. As she strode along the courthouse corridor, she towered over the rest of crowd and head after head swivelled as she marched to keep her appointment with justice.

Word spread quickly that a dominatrix was on trial in Courtroom 12 and the public benches soon filled with newspaper reporters and other spectators drawn in by the case. She embraced the attention. She hoped it would help people see the absurdity of it all, the waste of money and court time to prosecute somebody as insignificant as her.

It was a bitter disappointment when she discovered that the spectators and newspaper reporters were there only for salacious details and sexual adventure. Nobody seemed to care that she was being tried along with the rapists and the murderers.

Richard, or Det. Munro as she now knew him, took the stand the first day and recounted how he had visited her and negotiated to buy sex, or more precisely, anal penetration with a dildo. The assistant Crown attorney then began introducing items seized from her house as evidence. The court clerk blushed and the judge smiled as dildo after dildo was entered as exhibits. The court personnel wore gloves as they handled the items and the strap-on dildos ignited vicious tittering in the courtroom.

After that, Det. Munro talked about the ledger book they had seized and told the judge that there were the names of more than 150 men inside, along with summaries of the appointments and what they wanted. The judge shook his head as Det. Munro read out entries like "Phillip. 2 p.m. Foot fetish" or "Jonathan. 6 p.m. Golden shower."

The next day she took the stand, embracing the opportunity to give her side of the story. Yes, she admitted, she did provide services to men for money, but it wasn't prostitution. There wasn't any physical contact at all for the first several appointments and then the contact was more therapeutic than sexual. If a man simply wants sex, she testified, they will go to an escort service or cruise for hookers.

The judge asked for a week to consider his decision. Her lawyer told her to expect the worst, but the worst wouldn't be that bad. Sure enough, when the judge returned it was with a guilty verdict and a fine. It was only $500—an hour or two worth of spanking and whipping, noted some of the newspapers—but the conviction still stung. She thought the judge was compromising. The $500 fine showed he didn't consider the offence to be serious, but he didn't have the courage to stand up and say so by acquitting her.

What neither she nor her lawyer foresaw was the Revenue Canada investigation. While on the witness stand she had been asked to estimate her annual income and she had provided a rough guess of $100,000. Her trial was widely reported and that figure caught the eye of an auditor who wondered if she was declaring that income and paying the appropriate taxes. She wasn't.

With auditors about to descend and her name in the newspapers, she decided it was a good time to disappear.

$ $ $

On a warm winter day with the icicles forming puddles on the sidewalks, the moving vans arrived to cart away her belongings. She'd packed up her dungeon herself to avoid uncomfortable questions. A curious mover asked about the cage and she told him about her recently deceased German shepherd.

After the moving van pulled away, she slipped into her car and headed downtown to the police station. The officers had told her she could pick up her belongings, but she didn't want most of it, not after it had been in police hands. She did ask for the pair of red leather boots they'd seized as evidence though. The boots had cost $600 in New York and she wasn't willing to part with them.

I don't really need much else, she said. Earlier that week she'd visited one of the city's sex shops to replace her supply of dildos, strap-ons and handcuffs. It had been a fun shopping spree and the owner of the store gave her a tidy little discount because he recognized her from the newspaper.

Since her mother had moved to Florida years ago and she had no close friends in the city, she didn't mind leaving. Change was good. Some of her clients were upset, traumatized actually. They'd seen nobody else for years and there would be a vacuum to fill. After all, a good dominatrix is hard to find. She tut-tutted them and told them she would send them a postcard when she got settled. If they were that desperate, they could fly in for a visit. For her favourites, she gave them a deluxe last session for free which helped ease their pain.

Her last stop before leaving was her favourite coffee shop for one last cappuccino. Earlier, she'd been to the magazine store and picked up one of the tabloids from the city she was moving to. As she sprinkled cinnamon into her mug, she flipped the paper open to its back pages.

There were hundreds of sex ads offering everything from women who posed as school girls to muscular young men to Russian twins who provided threesomes. There was one column filled with ads for various domination services. With her long fingernail, she ran down the column, seeing what names were being used. She smiled when she saw there was already a Mistress Alexandra.

I wasn't going to use that again anyway, she said with a bit of a giggle.

There was one favour she wanted to ask before leaving. She wanted everybody involved with her case—all those police officers and lawyers—to know that although she was leaving the city, she wasn't leaving the business.

"I just want them to know I'm still alive and kicking." Then, with another glance at the sex ads in the back of the tabloid, she added, "And I'm not alone."

CONCLUSION

On April 19, 1999, a 29-year-old drug addict named Richard Hamilton staggered into a Harvey's restaurant and stumbled towards the counter. He'd been drinking and coking all day long and as the young woman behind the cash looked into his reddened eyes, she sensed there would be trouble.

At first, Hamilton did nothing wrong. Slurring his words terribly, he managed to order a hamburger, no fries, and a glass of water. The problem started when the cashier asked for the $2.88 he owed for the meal. Hamilton dug his hands into his pockets and mumbled something about having no money.

Slightly bewildered, the cashier repeated her request. Hamilton dug into his pockets once more and this time pulled out a tarnished and scratched .32 calibre Smith and Wesson bullet.

According to the cashier, Hamilton then let loose with a series of grunts that sounded roughly like "Give me your money." To be honest, she couldn't be sure of exactly what he said; Hamilton was so drunk and incoherent, his words ran into one another, creating a confusing stream of sound.

Not wanting to trigger a serious crisis, the cashier handed Hamilton the contents of the register, a little more than $200 in total. He stumbled out of the restaurant and the cashier quickly called 911.

When police arrived, they rewound the security tape and got a good look at their suspect: a white man wearing khakis and a Boston Bruins sweatshirt with a hood. Less than 30 minutes later, Hamilton was picked up by a patrol unit outside a well-known crackhouse a few blocks from the Harvey's. He was still wearing his Bruins shirt, but half of his take had already been spent on drugs. When police searched his pockets, they found two bullets and no gun. He was arrested, driven down to the station, processed, and charged with armed robbery.

Faced with the damning evidence of the cashier's testimony, the videotape and the police arrest, when the case came to court ten weeks later, on June 30, 1999, Hamilton had few options but to plead guilty. With his long criminal record featuring three previous convictions for robbery, the judge showed little sympathy. He was sentenced to two-and-a-half years and sent directly to a federal penitentiary.

"Mr. Hamilton wasn't born into the same privileges that you or I have enjoyed. This is a man who was born into petty, meaningless and self-destructive crime," said James Foord, Hamilton's lawyer. "It's disheartening to see society put its resources into a prison term instead of getting to the root of these problems. It was simply a stupid act. It was a drunken, desperate act fuelled by his addiction to cocaine."

It was also an incredibly common act, at least in terms of thoughtfulness and execution.

When I started covering crime for the newspaper, I was on the police beat. That meant my job was to write about breaking police stories—murders, rapes, drunk driving accidents, and a myriad of senseless road fatalities. My daily routine was to call different units of the police department on the hour to see if anything was going on and to respond to police press releases about their latest arrest or the most recent suspect they were looking for. The whole time, a police scanner would crackle in the background and I would keep one ear open for the tell-tale sounds of a police chase in progress or a 911 call reporting gun shots or the ever-scintillating request for a coroner to attend the scene of a crime.

During my time as a police reporter, it was only the most major crimes that would come to my attention—the murders, the high-end drug dealers, the ring of roof-top break-and-enter experts. These are the calls I paid attention to on the scanner, these are the calls the police told me about on the phone, and these are the calls that police thought were worthy of press releases. As for the dozens of daily car thefts and break-and-enters and common assaults, they were never even mentioned or paid attention to because they were simply "routine."

Because all I saw were these high-end crimes, it began to taint my image of criminals. The people I wrote about, the criminals I actually met were people like Simon, Ian, and Josh. Eccentric marijuana advocates, thrilling safe crackers, and adrenaline-filled car thieves. After a while, I almost expected all criminals to be flashy, or passionate, or at least dark and scheming. It was from that mindset that this book idea came to me.

I thought it would be fascinating to write in-depth about these criminals I was meeting through my work at the newspaper. I enjoyed researching and writing my first true crime book, *The Champagne Gang*, and I wanted to learn more about this segment of our community—who they are, how they got here, and how they did the things that got them here. With that in mind, *Money For Nothing* was born.

Then, before I actually started on the book, I switched jobs. One of the *Ottawa Citizen*'s court reporters accepted an offer from the newly founded *National Post*. I applied for the open position and in October 1998, I reported to the Ottawa courthouse.

With 36 courtrooms spread out over three floors at the Elgin Street building, I got to see a lot of criminals pass through the system. I quickly learned the vast majority weren't unique characters like Simon or charismatic like Ian or plain-old neurotic like Josh. Most were people like Richard Hamilton—desperate people from this country's considerable underclass who are forced, through addiction, or dire poverty, or mental illness, to go out and commit stupid crimes with no thought to the consequences. Day after day, you see them paraded in and out of the courts and in and out of the cells, all with a very common background: very little education, very little family support growing up, and way too much alcohol and cocaine and violence in their life. When somebody different does come around—like Ken, the Locker Room Bandit—it's almost shocking to see the contrast.

After my first months in the courthouse, I began to regret the image of criminals I was presenting in this book. While the nine men and one woman I've spent time with and written about are interesting, charismatic, self-analytical, and often intelligent, they are not the rule. They are the exception to hundreds of people like Richard Hamilton. They are the blue jays and the hummingbirds among a flock of common sparrows.

In the end, that is the lasting lesson I've learned from writing *Money for Nothing*. Everyone has a stereotypical image in their head of a criminal. Some picture black youths, some picture lazy welfare hoods, some picture Mafia types like they saw in the *Godfather* movies. I pictured them as eccentric, lovable characters.

Of course, in reality they are not. They're Richard Hamiltons, or they're violent men who beat their women, or they're tortured, perverted souls who prey on children, or they're rich and contented and smug and glide through the system after being charged with drunk driving. Then, on rare occasions, there are people like I've written about.

At the very least, this book changed my image of those who live their life on the other side of the law. Hopefully, in some small way, the portraits I've included here could change yours as well.

MORE RIVETING TALES OF TRUE CRIME

FROM WARWICK PUBLISHING

THE CHAMPAGNE GANG
High Times and Sweet Crimes

Jeremy Mercer

Money for Nothing author Mercer's first book tells the fast-paced story of a gang of young men who wanted the good life and worked out an incredibly successful—though illegal—way to get it, pulling off one of the most lucrative string of robberies ever perpetrated nationwide.

(ISBN 1-895629-97-7)

THE SEVENTH SHADOW
The Wilderness Manhunt for a Brutal Mass Murderer

RCMP Sgt. (Ret.) Michael Eastham,
with Ian McLeod

The tragic story of one of Canada's worst mass murder cases and the relentless hunt to catch the killer, fully told for the first time by the man who led the investigation.

(ISBN 1-894020-47-2)

We hope you have enjoyed this book.

Please send us your comments and suggestions.

Warwick Publishing
162 John Street
Toronto, Ontario
M5V 2E5
Canada

Telephone: (416) 596-1555

E-mail: mbrooke@warwickgp.com

Please visit us on the Web at

www.warwickgp.com